PIANO • VOCAL • GUITAR

ELVIS PRESLEY

HIS COUNTRY HITS

CONTENTS

ISBN 978-0-634-01479-6

7777 W. Bluemound Rd. P.O. Box 13819 Milwaukee, WI 53213

www.elvis.com

Visit Hal Leonard Online at
www.halleonard.com

DON'T

Words and Music by JERRY LEIBER
and MIKE STOLLER

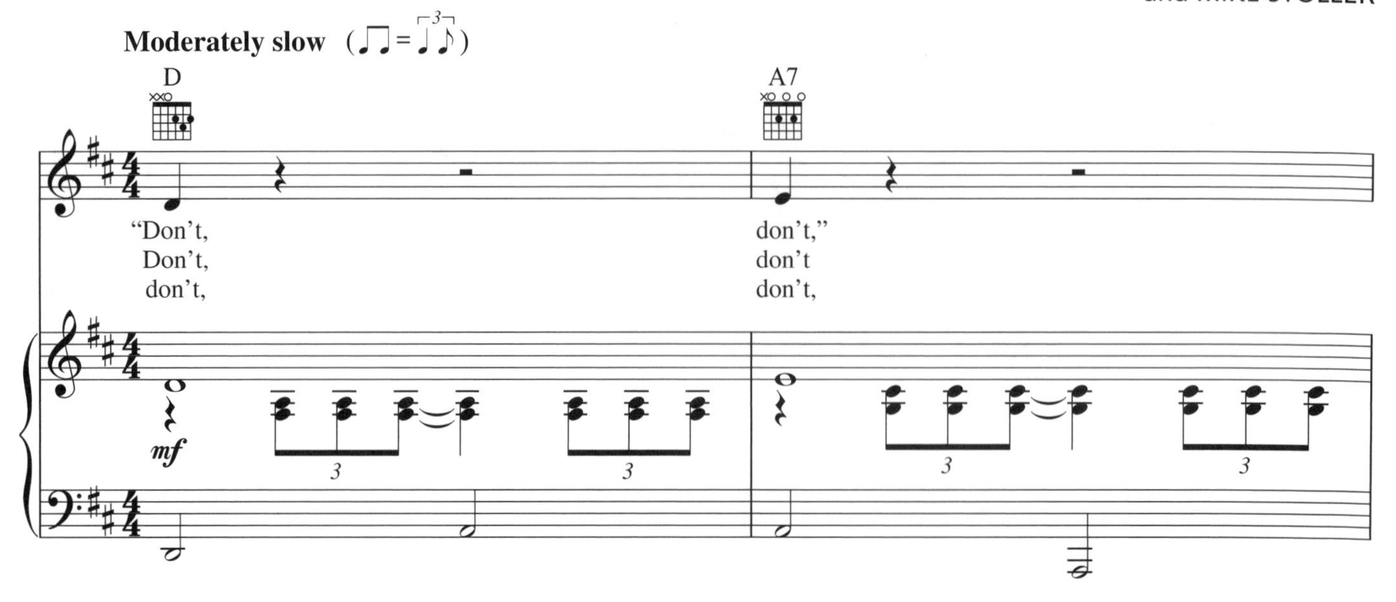

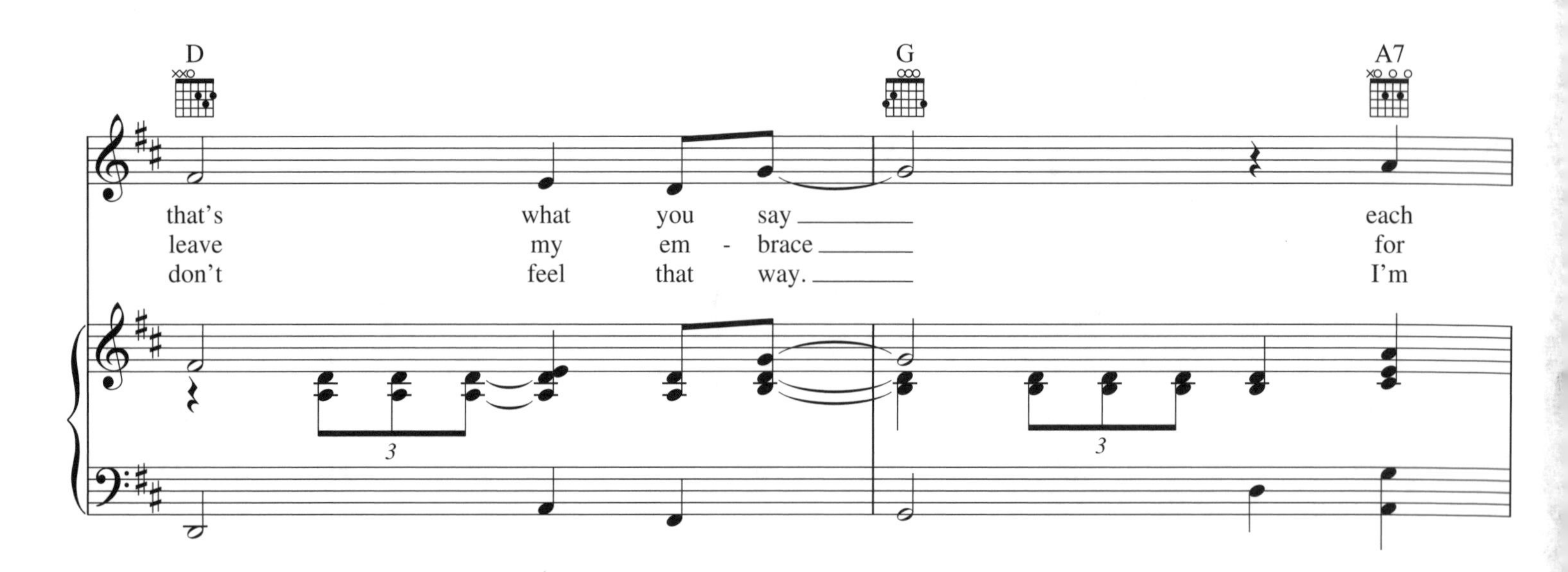

Em7
A7
way.
place.
stay.
When I feel like
When the night grows
This you can be -
D
D7
G
Em7
G/A
To Coda
3fr
this and I want to kiss you, ba - by, don't say
cold and I want to hold you, ba - by, don't say
lieve, I will nev - er leave you. Heav - en knows I
1
D
Em7
G/A
A
"don't."
2
D
D7
Am7
D7
G
"don't."
If you think that

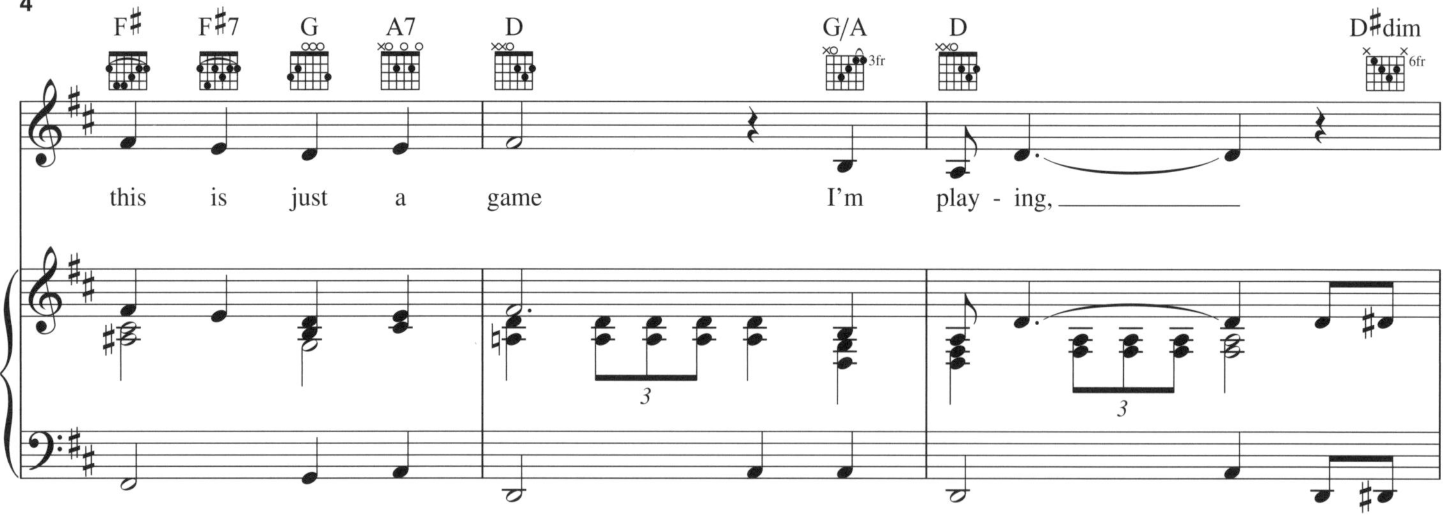
F♯ F♯7 G A7 D G/A D D♯dim
3fr
6fr
this is just a game I'm play - ing,
3
3

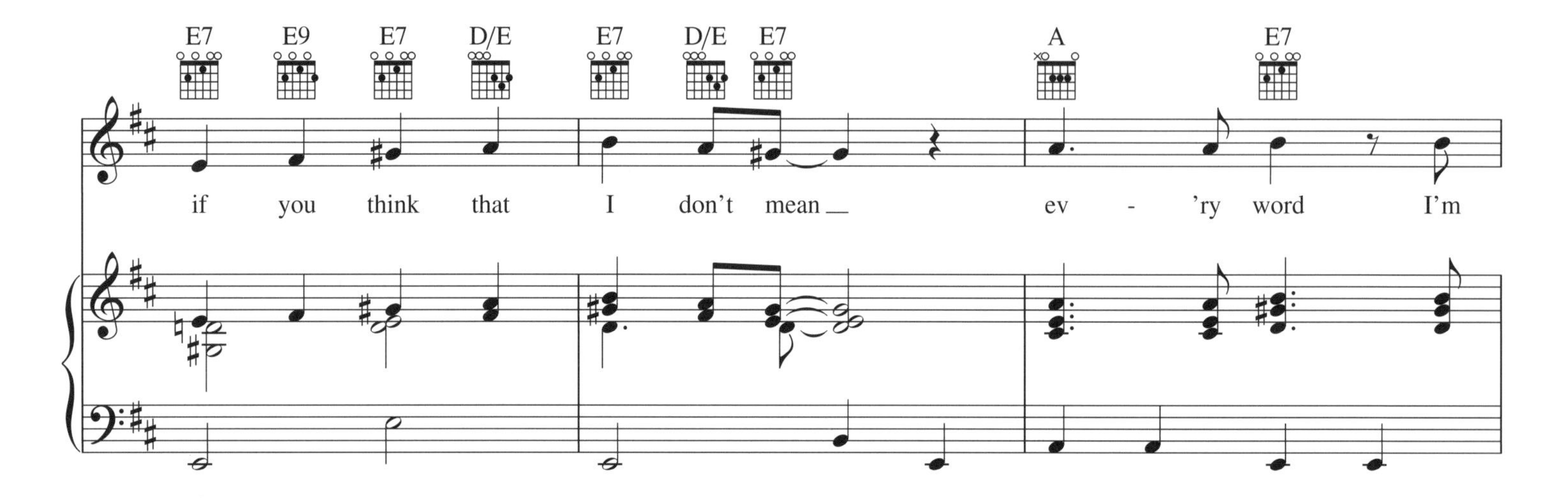
E7 E9 E7 D/E E7 D/E E7 A E7
if you think that I don't mean ev - 'ry word I'm

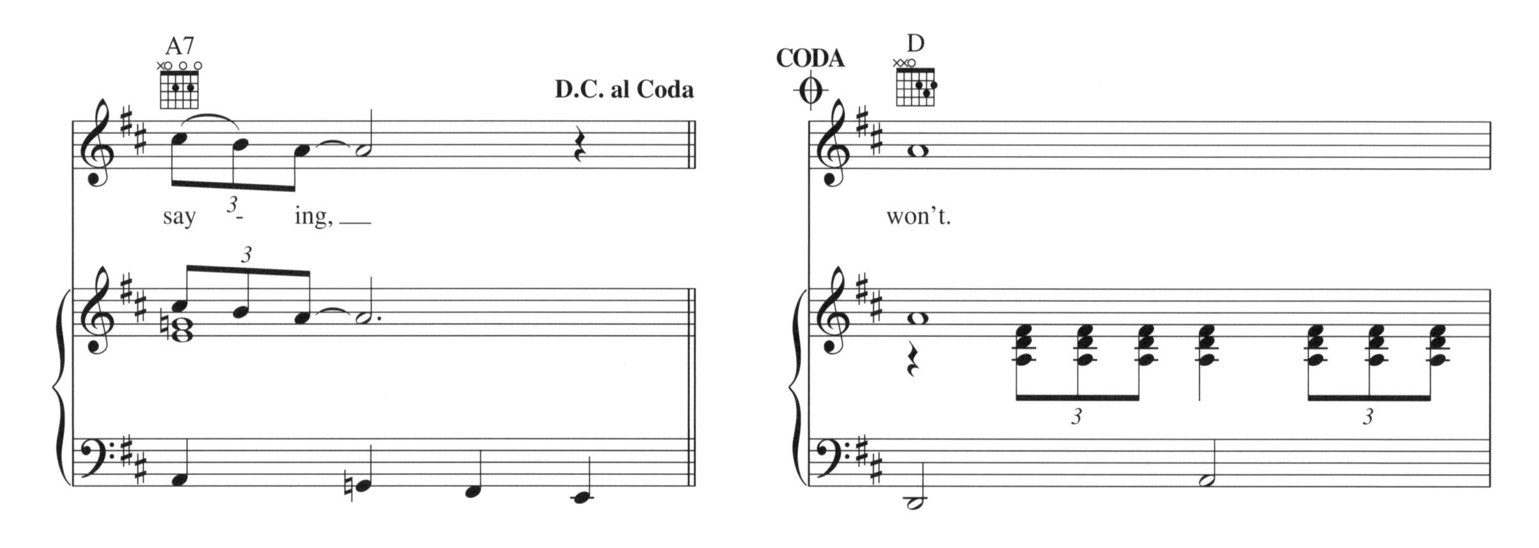
A7
D.C. al Coda
CODA
D
say - ing,
won't.
3
3
3

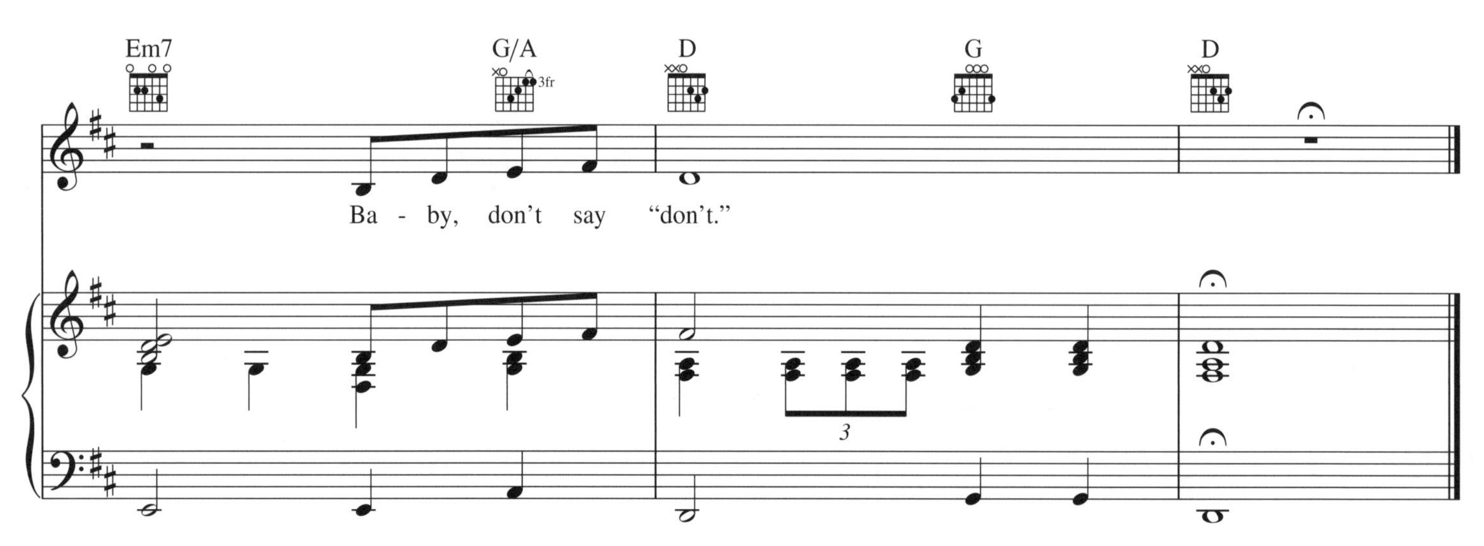
Em7 G/A D G D
3fr
Ba - by, don't say "don't."
3

ALL SHOOK UP

Words and Music by OTIS BLACKWELL
and ELVIS PRESLEY

Eb7
F7
Bb
Eb7
mm oh, oh, yeah, yeah!

Bb
My hands are shak - y and my knees are weak, I

can't seem to stand on my own two feet. Who do you thank when you

have such luck? I'm in love! I'm all shook up! Mm

E♭7
F7
B♭
E♭7
mm oh, oh, yeah, yeah!

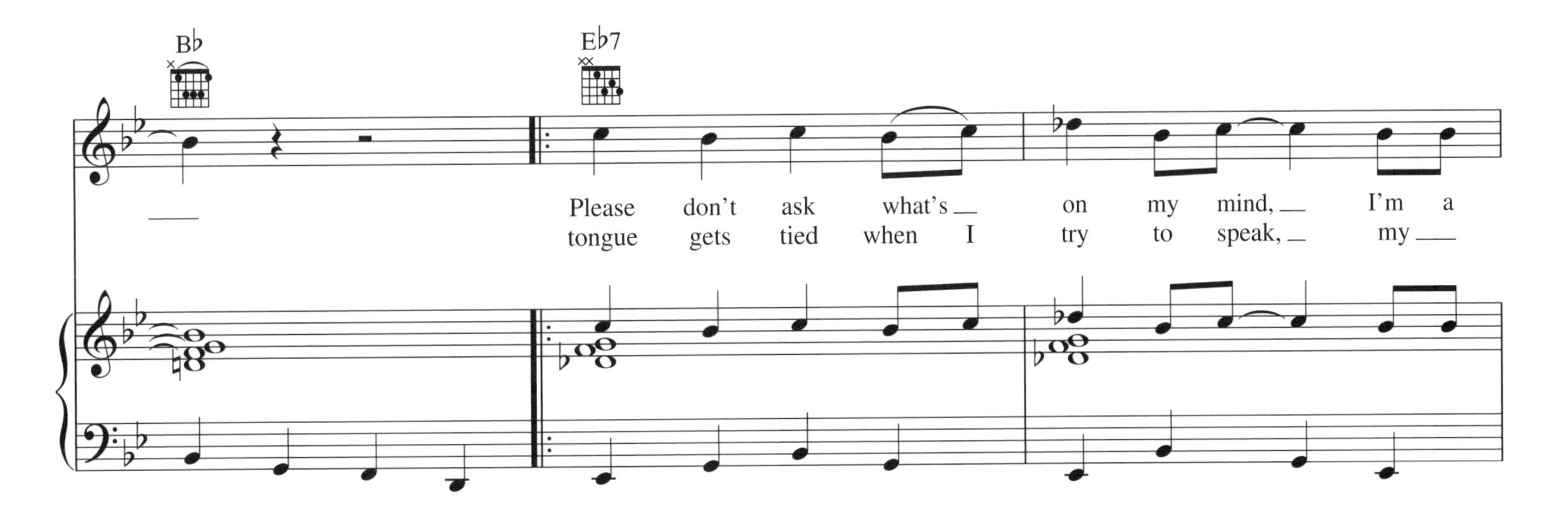
B♭
E♭7
Please don't ask what's on my mind, I'm a
tongue gets tied when I try to speak, my

B♭
lit - tle mixed up but I'm feel - in' fine. When I'm
in - sides shake like a leaf on a tree. There's

E♭7
near that girl that I love best, my
on - ly one cure for this soul of mine, that's to

F7
B♭
heart beats so it scares me to death!
have the girl that I love so fine!
She touched my hand, what a
chill I got, her kiss - es are like a vol - ca - no that's hot! I'm
proud to say she's my but - ter - cup. I'm in love! I'm
E♭7
F7
all shook up! Mm mm oh, oh, yeah,

1
2
B♭
E♭7
B♭
B♭
yeah!
My
yeah!
I'm

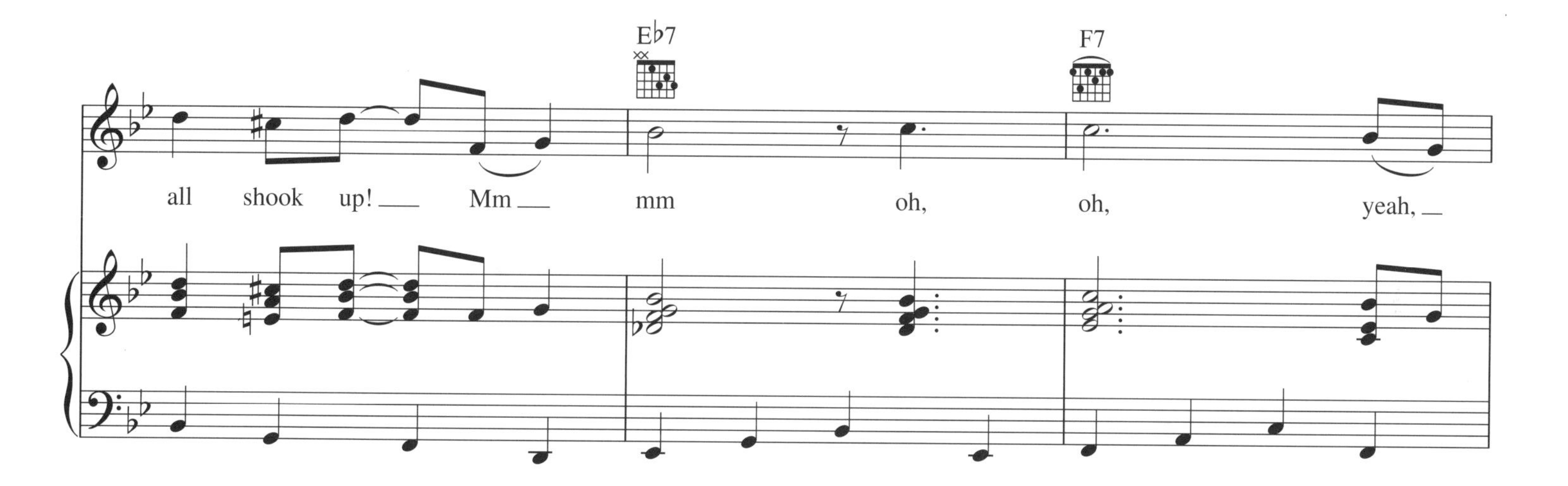
E♭7
F7
all shook up! Mm mm oh, oh, yeah,

B♭
E♭7
yeah! I'm all shook up! Mm mm oh,

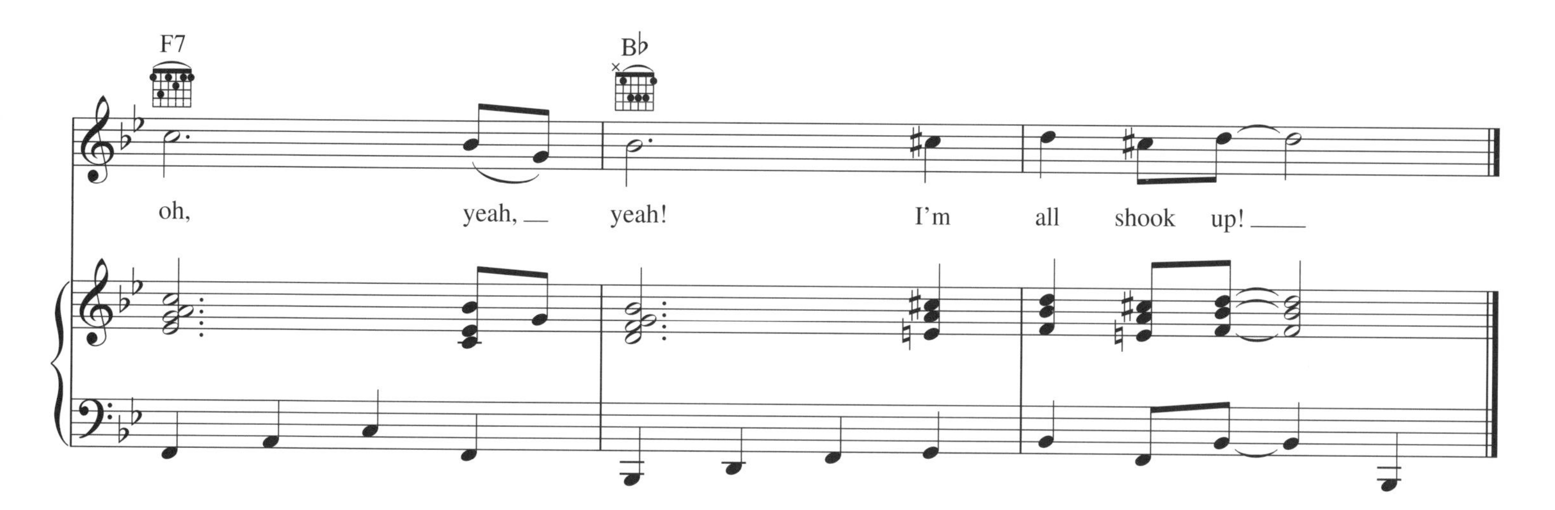
F7
B♭
oh, yeah, yeah! I'm all shook up!

BABY, LET'S PLAY HOUSE

Written by ARTHUR GUNTER

Additional Lyrics

3. This is one thing, baby
   What I want you to know:
   Come on back and let's play a little house
   So we can do what we did before.
   Chorus

4. Listen, I'm telling you, baby,
   Don't you understand?
   I'd rather see you dead, little girl,
   Than to be with another man.
   Chorus

DON'T BE CRUEL
(To a Heart That's True)

Words and Music by OTIS BLACKWELL
and ELVIS PRESLEY

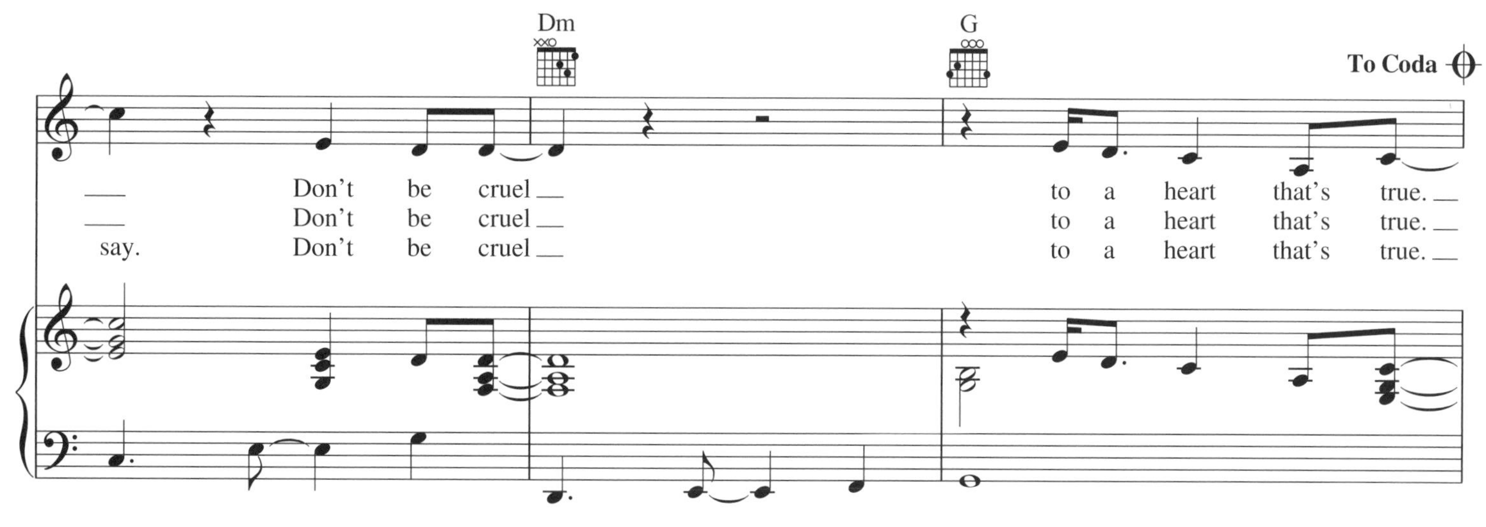
Dm
G
To Coda
Don't be cruel to a heart that's true.
Don't be cruel to a heart that's true.
say. Don't be cruel to a heart that's true.

C
1
2, 3
(2.) I don't

F
G
F
want no oth - er love. Ba - by, it's just
Why should we be a - part, I real - ly, real - ly love you,

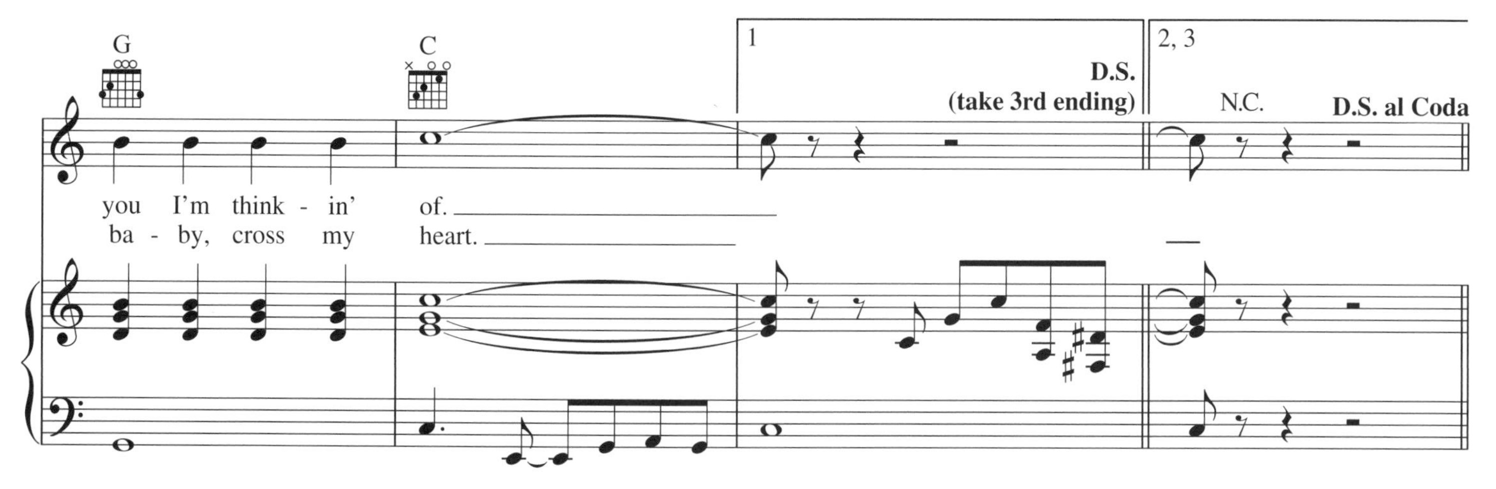
G
C
1
D.S.
(take 3rd ending)
2, 3
N.C.
D.S. al Coda
you I'm think - in' of.
ba - by, cross my heart.

CODA
C
A
Solo ends
Let's

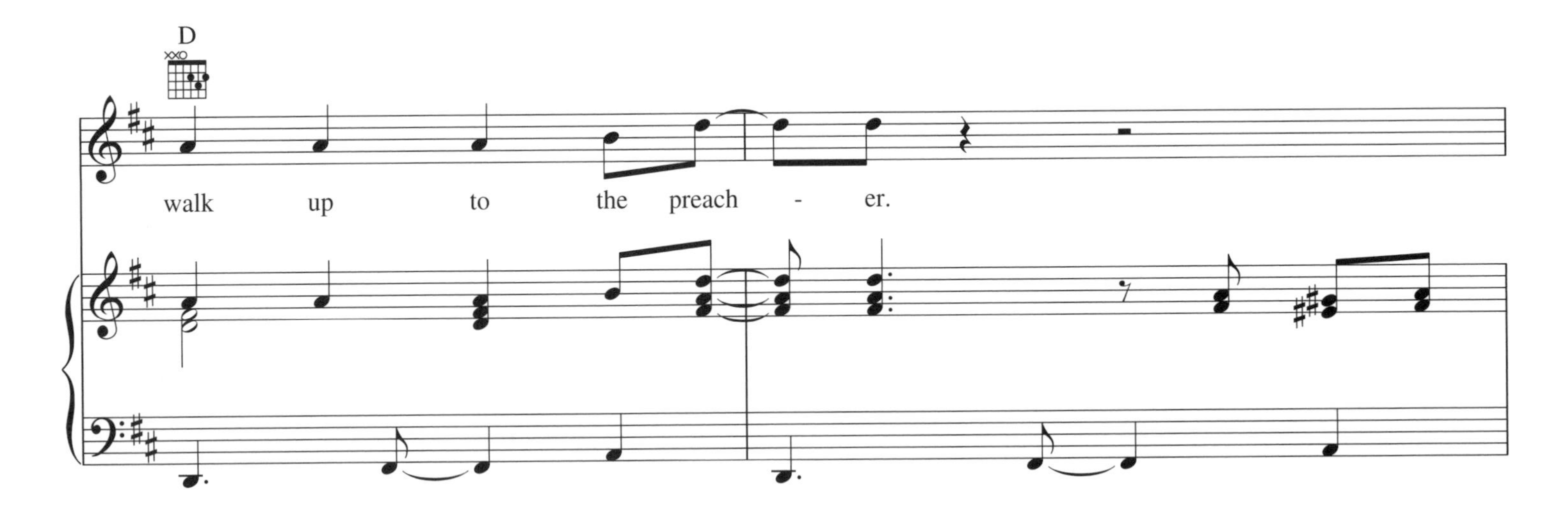

D
walk up to the preach - er.

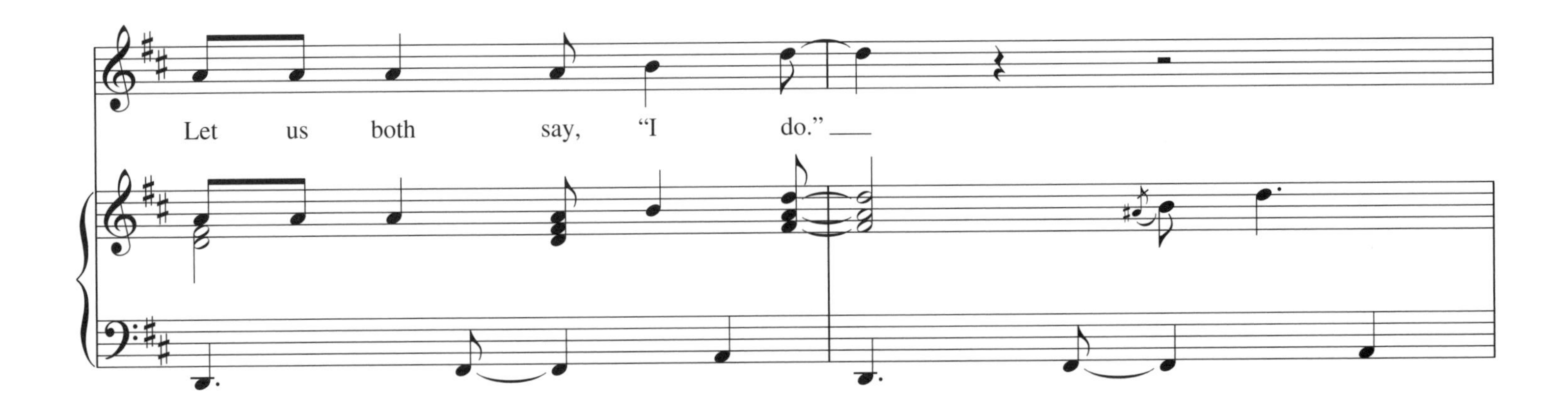

Let us both say, "I do."

G
Then you'll know you have me and

D
Em7
I know I'll have you, too.
Don't be cruel

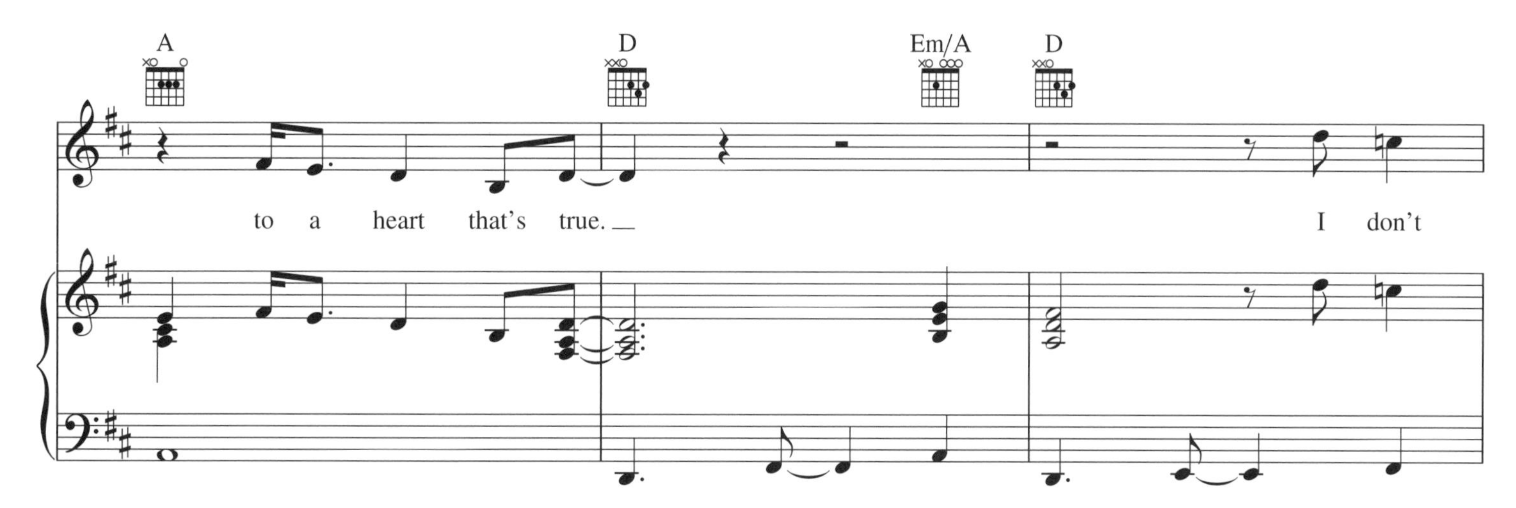
A
D
Em/A
D
to a heart that's true.
I don't

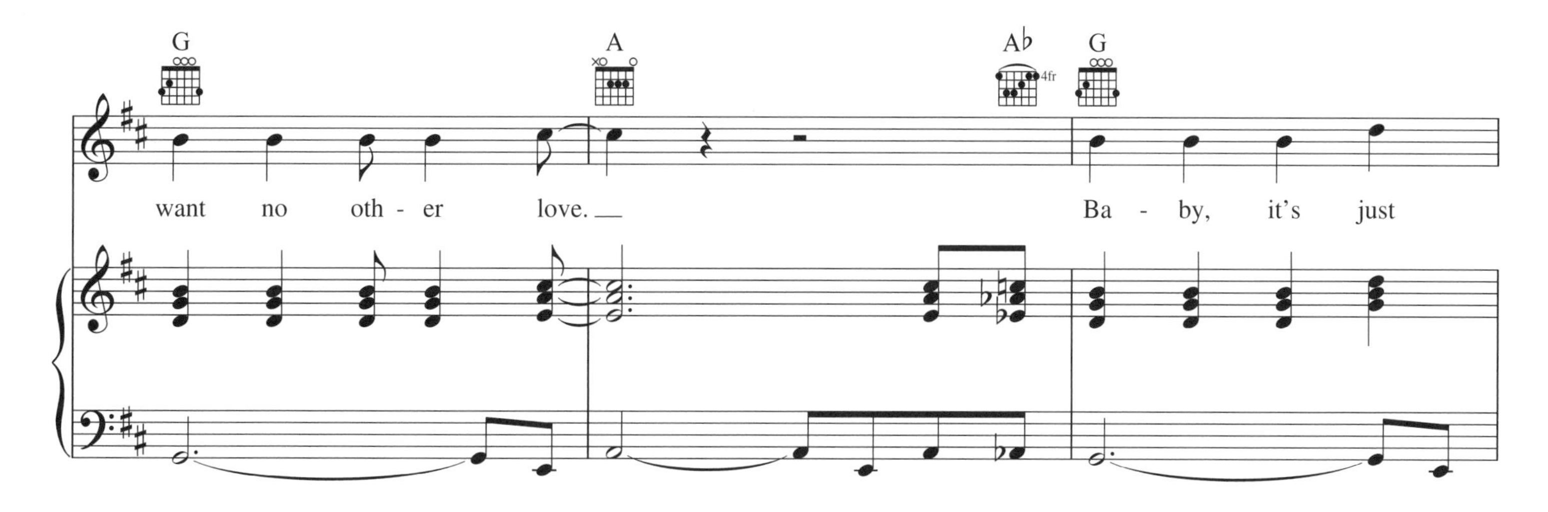
G
A
A♭
G
want no oth - er love.
Ba - by, it's just

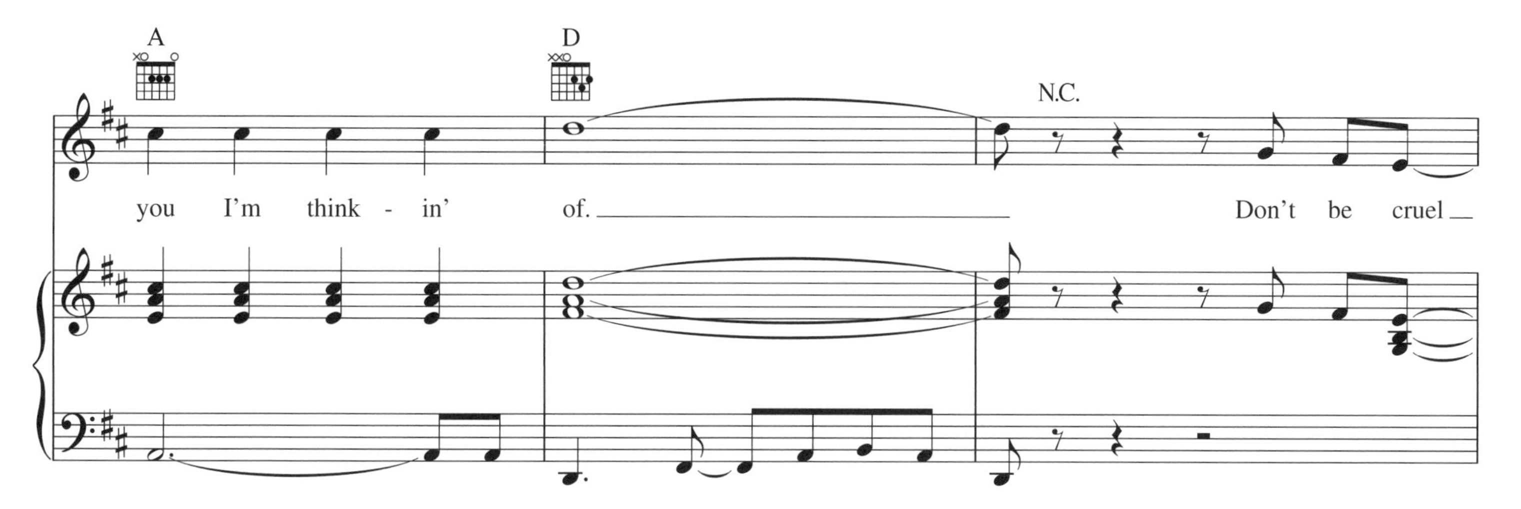
A
D
N.C.
you I'm think - in' of.
Don't be cruel

Em7
A
D
Em/A
to a heart that's true.

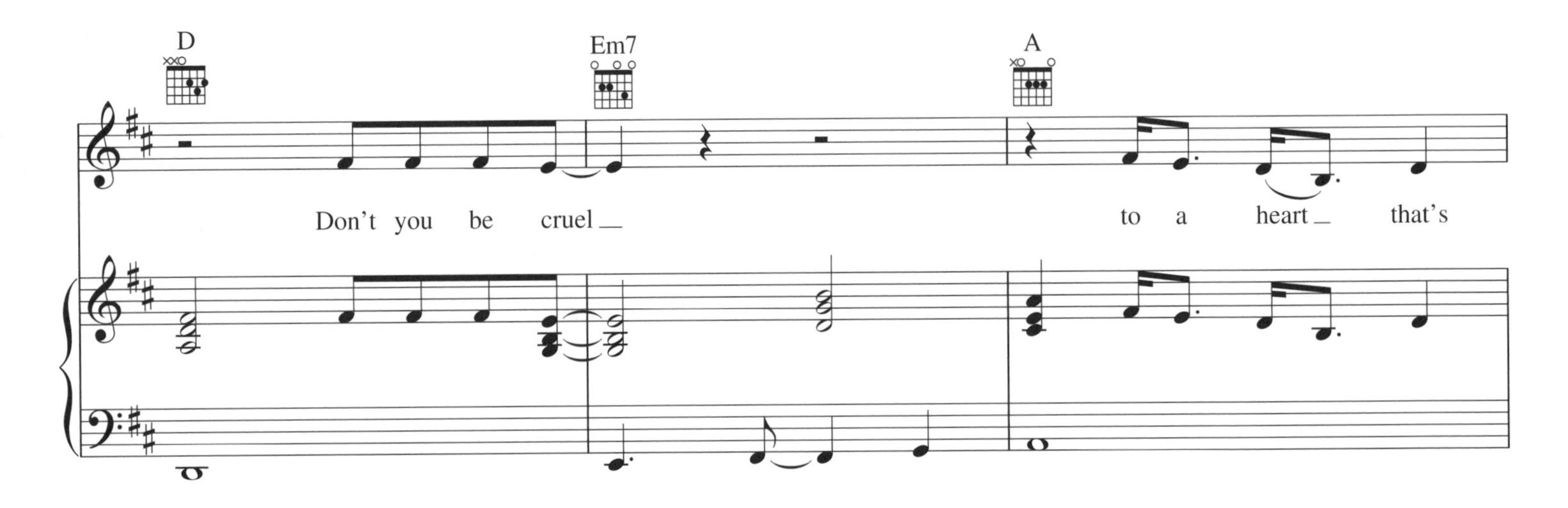
D
Em7
A
Don't you be cruel
to a heart that's

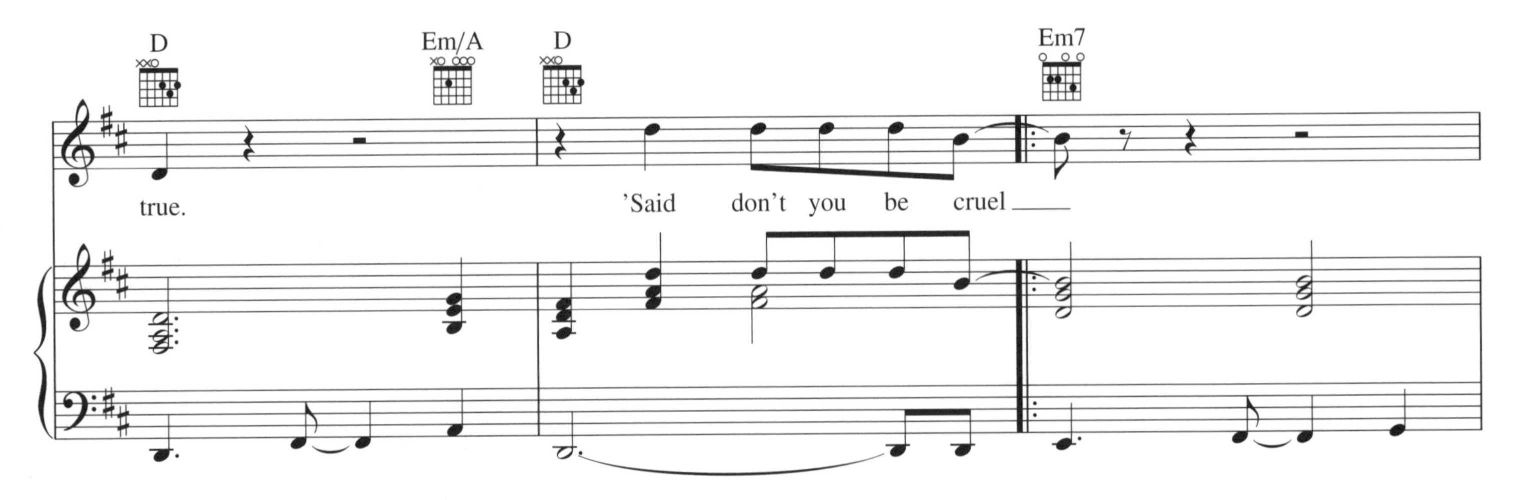
D
Em/A
D
Em7
true.
'Said don't you be cruel

A
D
Em/A
Repeat and Fade
D
Optional Ending
D
to a heart that's true.
No, don't be cruel

DON'T CRY DADDY

Words and Music by
MAC DAVIS

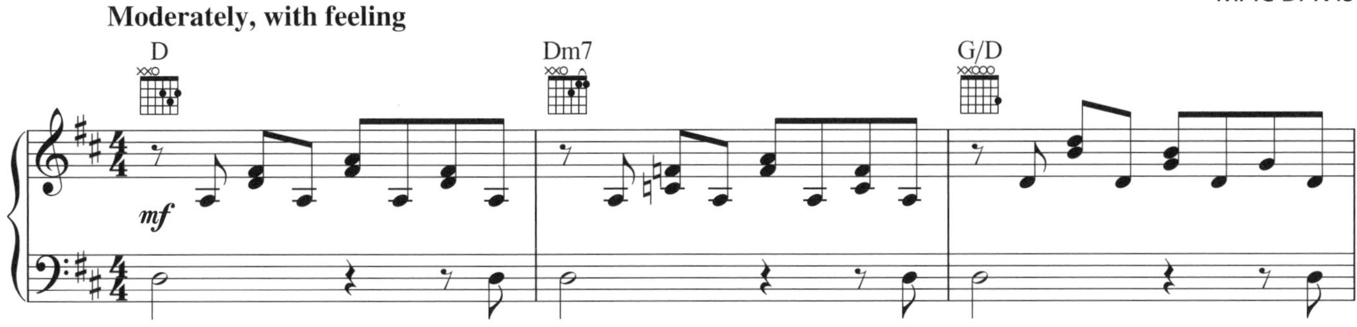

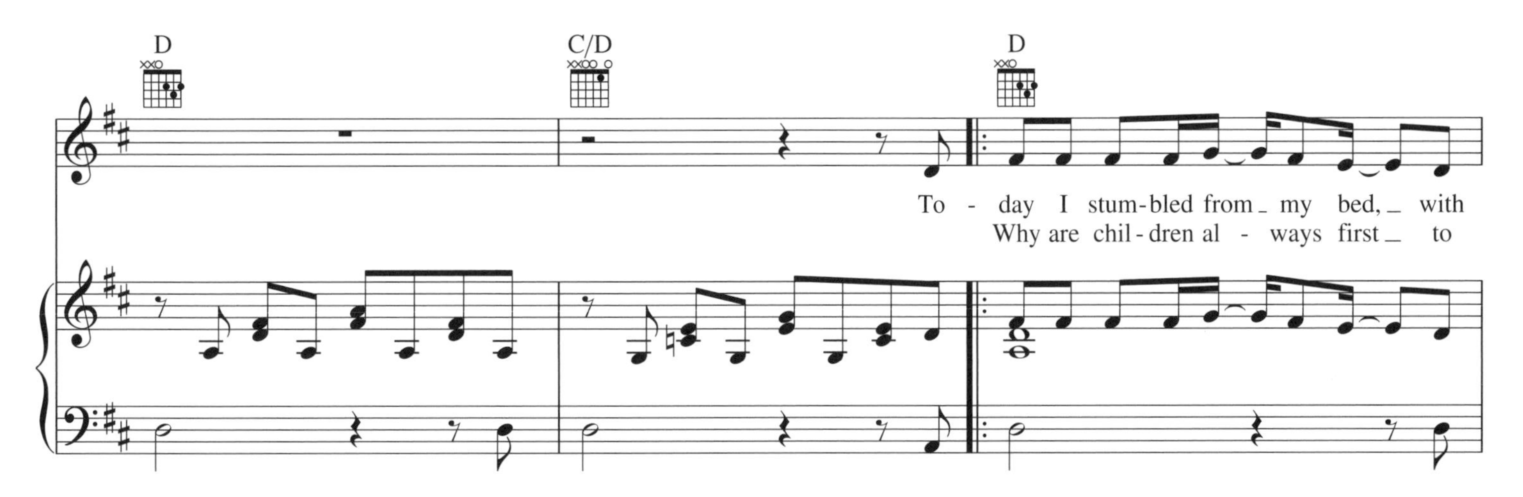

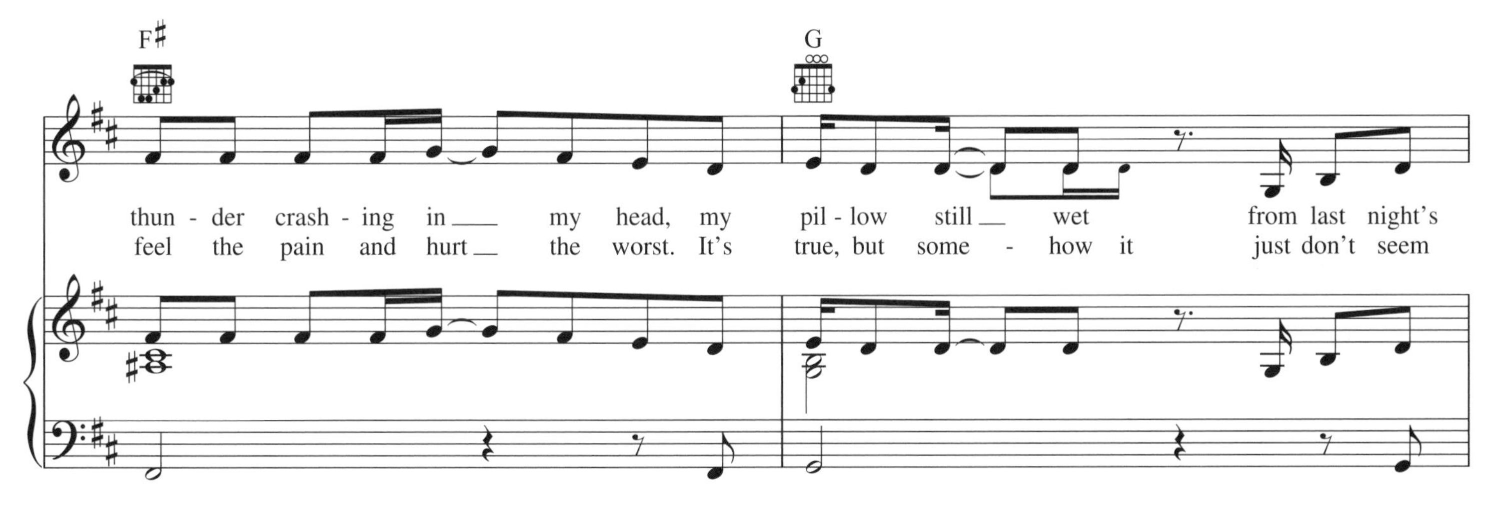

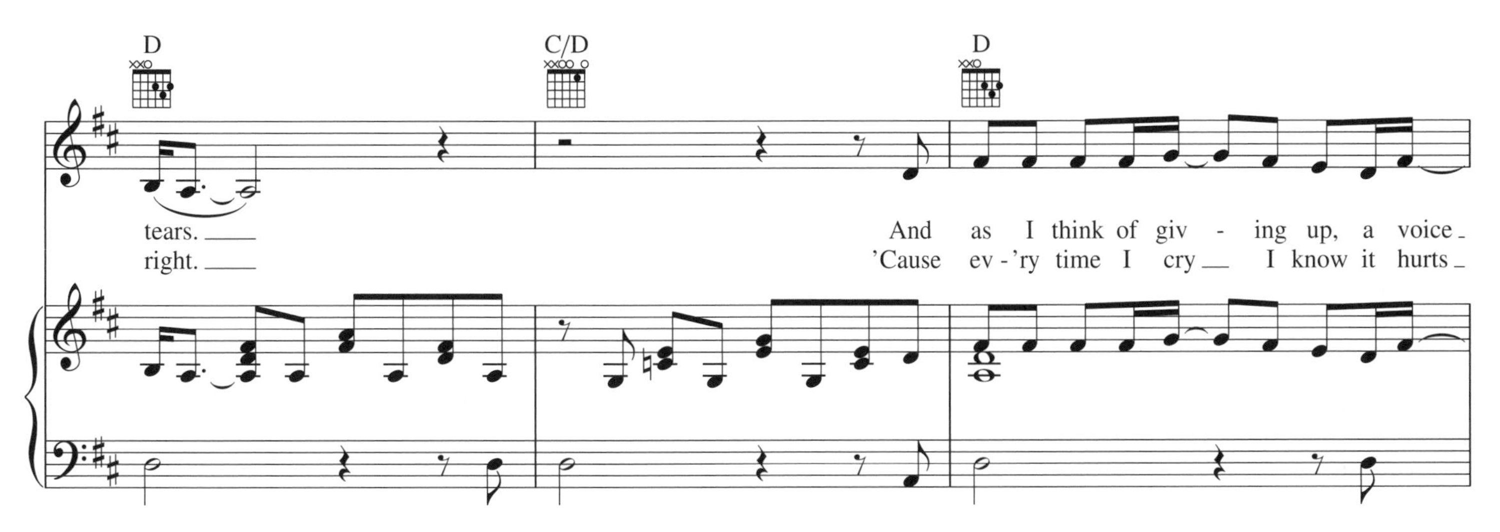

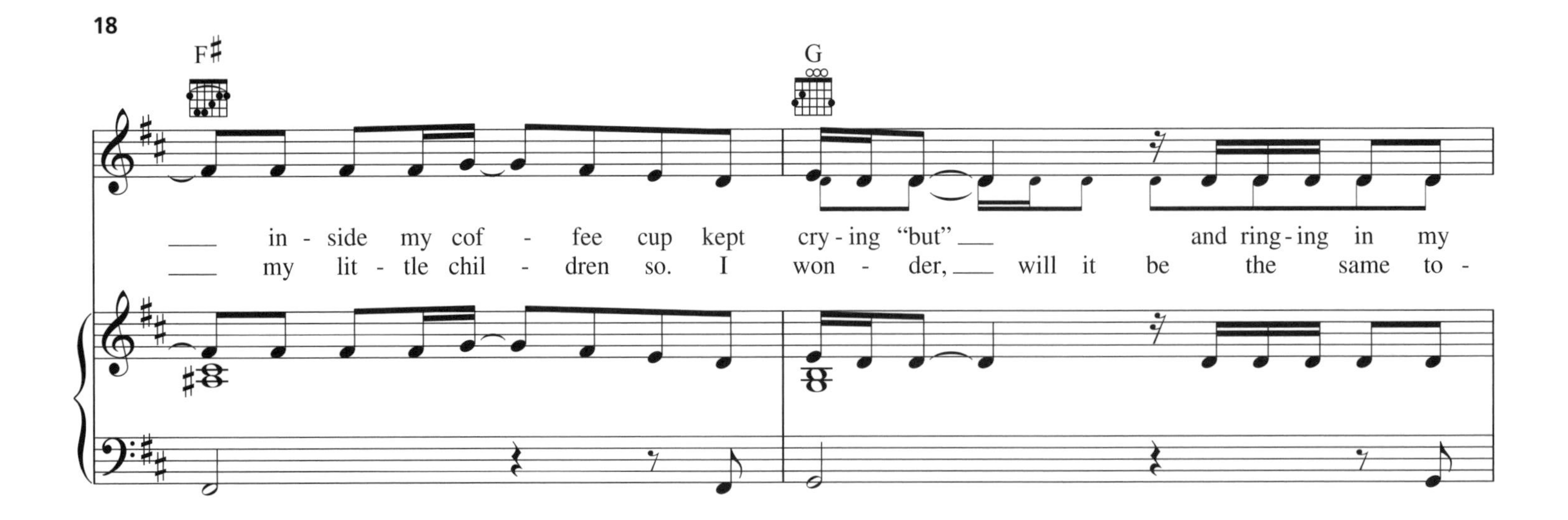
F♯
G
in - side my cof - fee cup kept cry - ing "but" and ring - ing in my
my lit - tle chil - dren so. I won - der, will it be the same to -

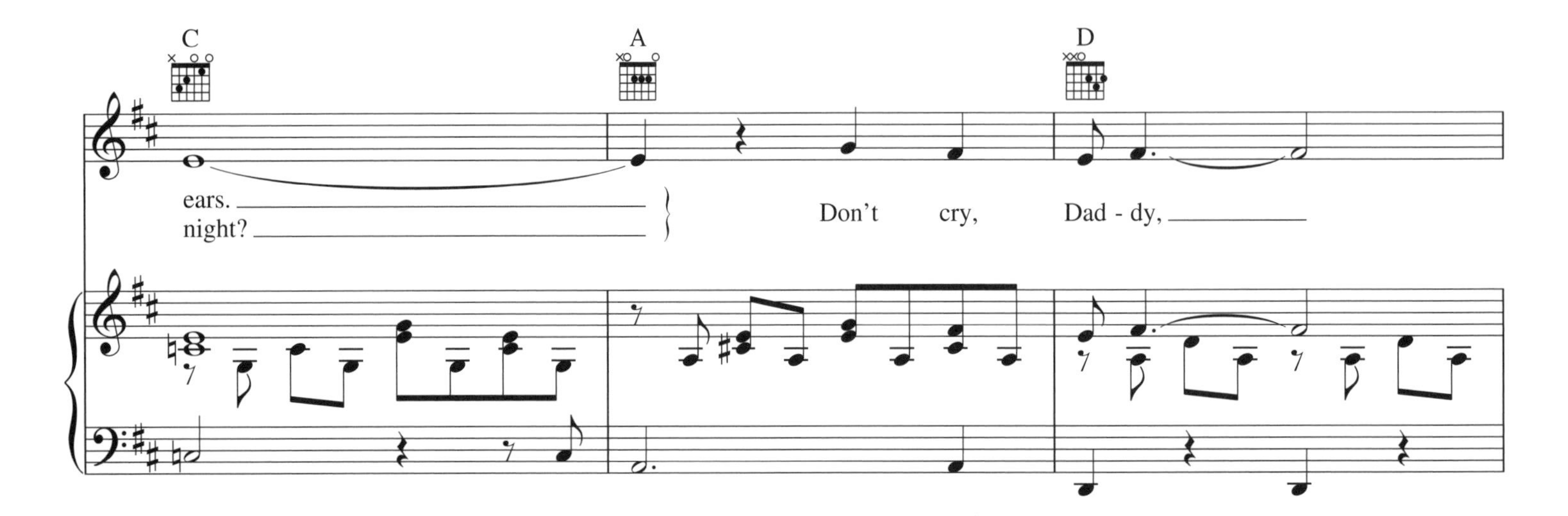
C
A
D
ears.
night?
Don't cry, Dad - dy,

Em
A
Dad - dy, please don't cry;
Dad - dy,

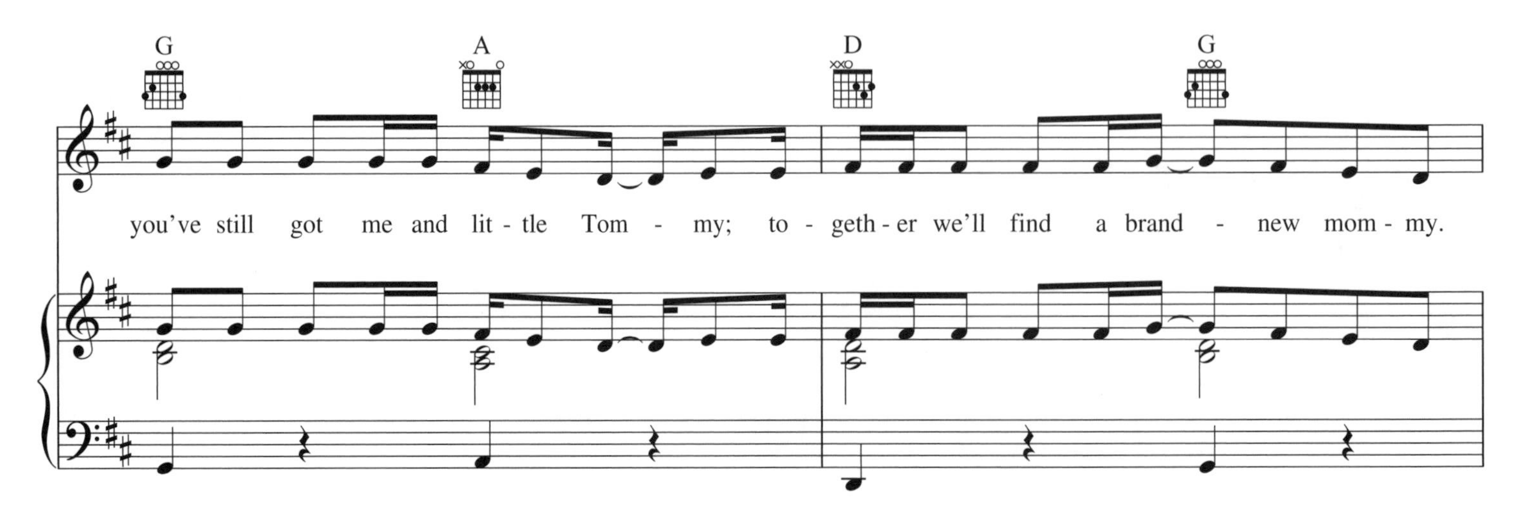
G
A
D
G
you've still got me and lit - tle Tom - my; to - geth - er we'll find a brand - new mom - my.

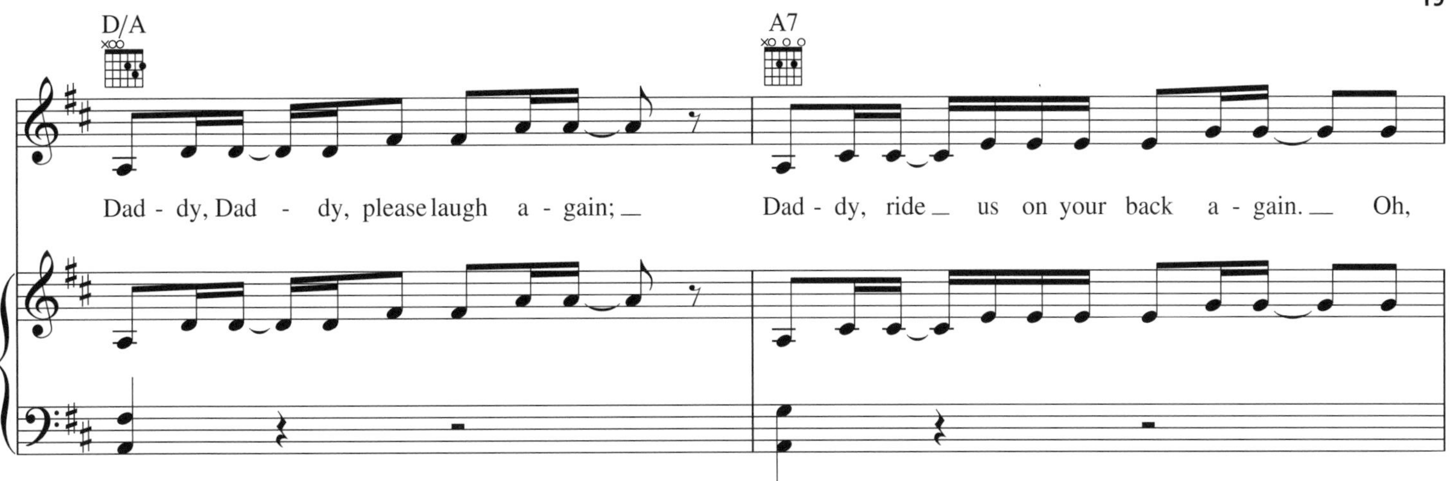
D/A
A7
Dad - dy, Dad - dy, please laugh a - gain;
Dad - dy, ride us on your back a - gain. Oh,

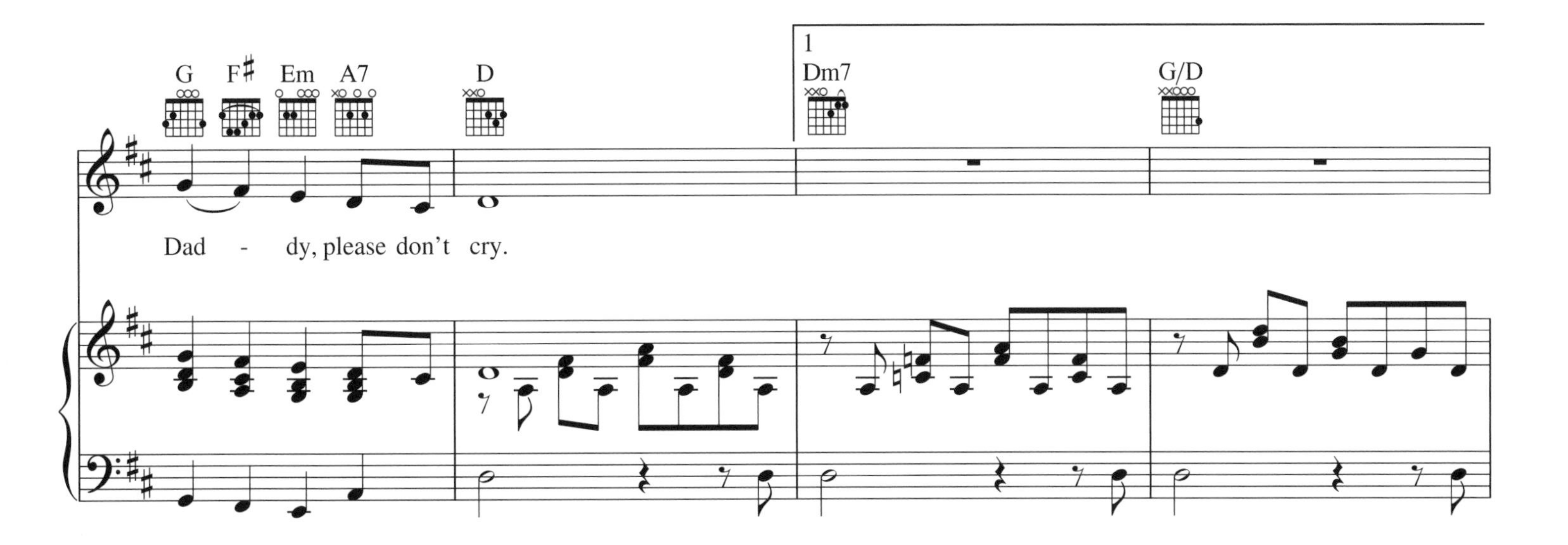
G F♯ Em A7 D
1
Dm7
G/D
Dad - dy, please don't cry.

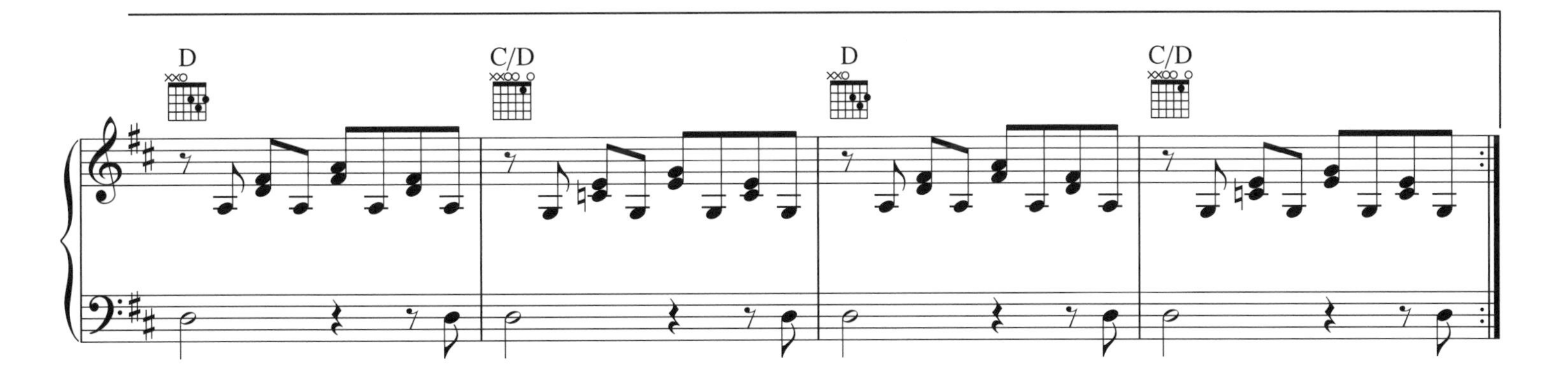
D
C/D
D
C/D

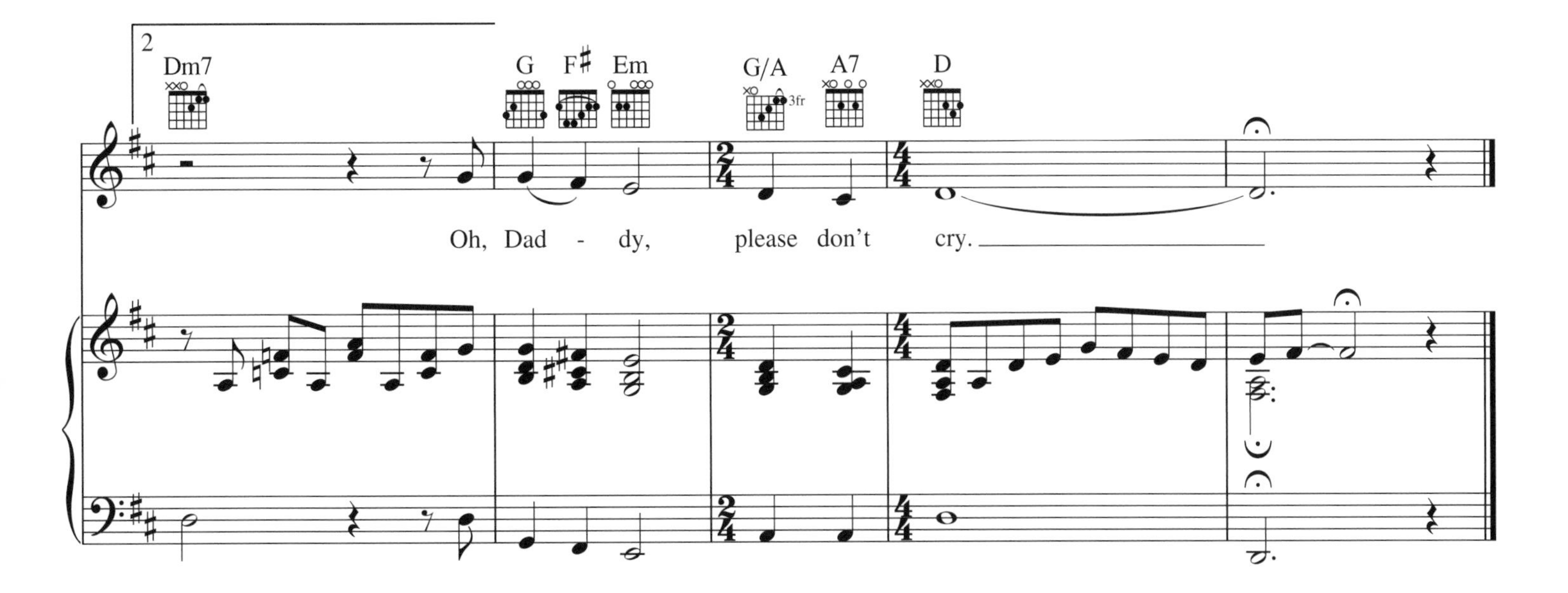
2
Dm7
G F♯ Em
G/A
3fr
A7
D
Oh, Dad - dy, please don't cry.

HARD HEADED WOMAN

Words and Music by
CLAUDE DeMETRUIS

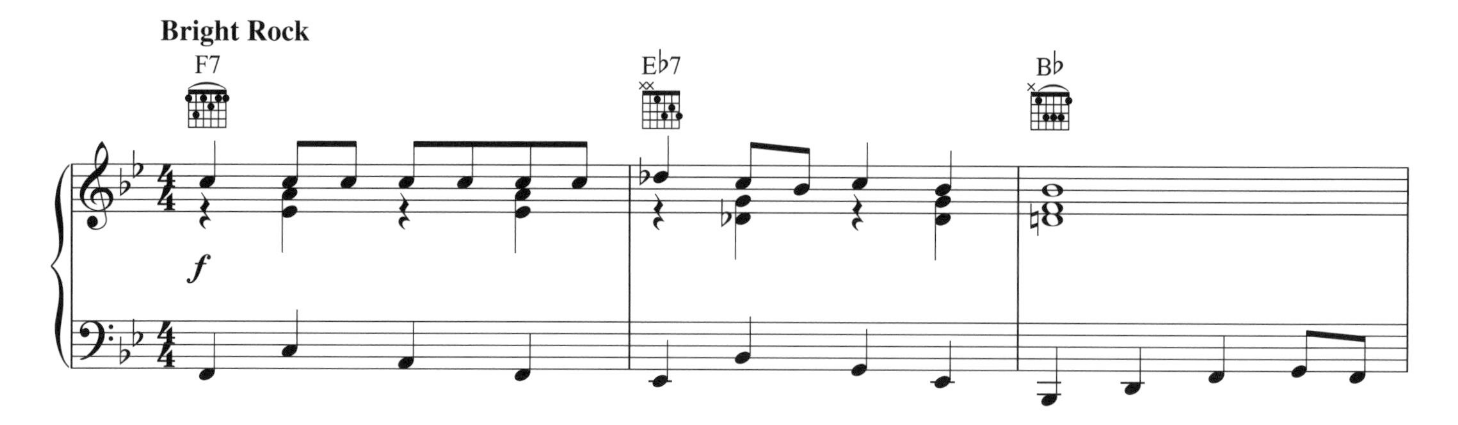

E♭7
B♭
yeah,
ev - er since the world be - gan,
uh - huh huh,

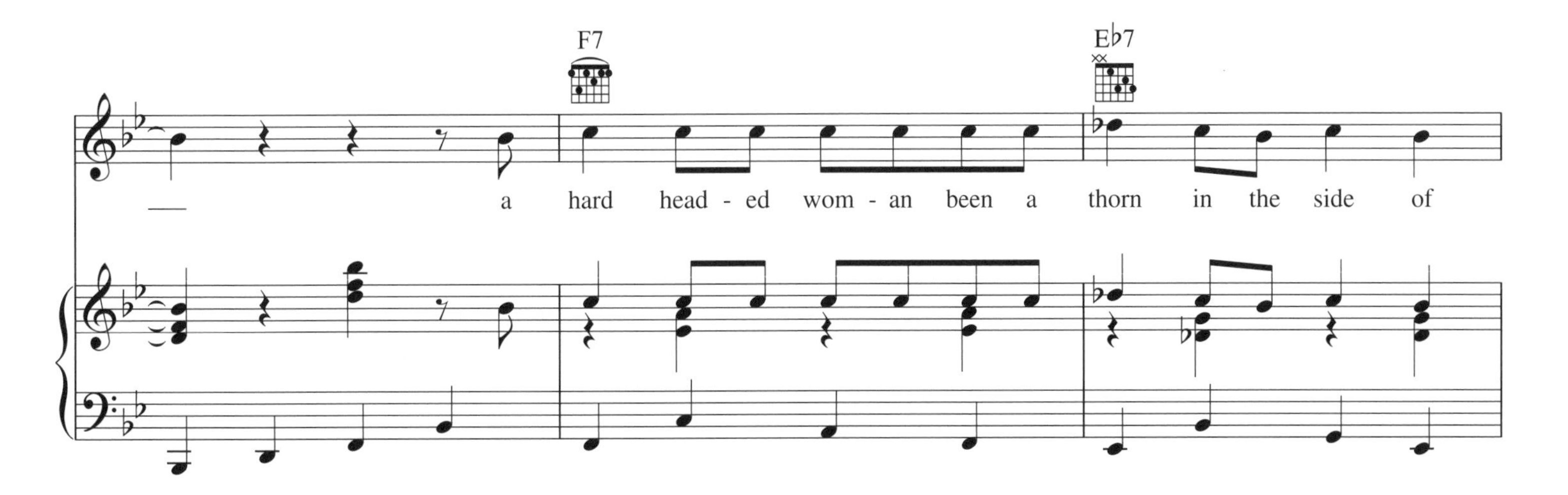
F7
E♭7
a hard head - ed wom - an been a thorn in the side of

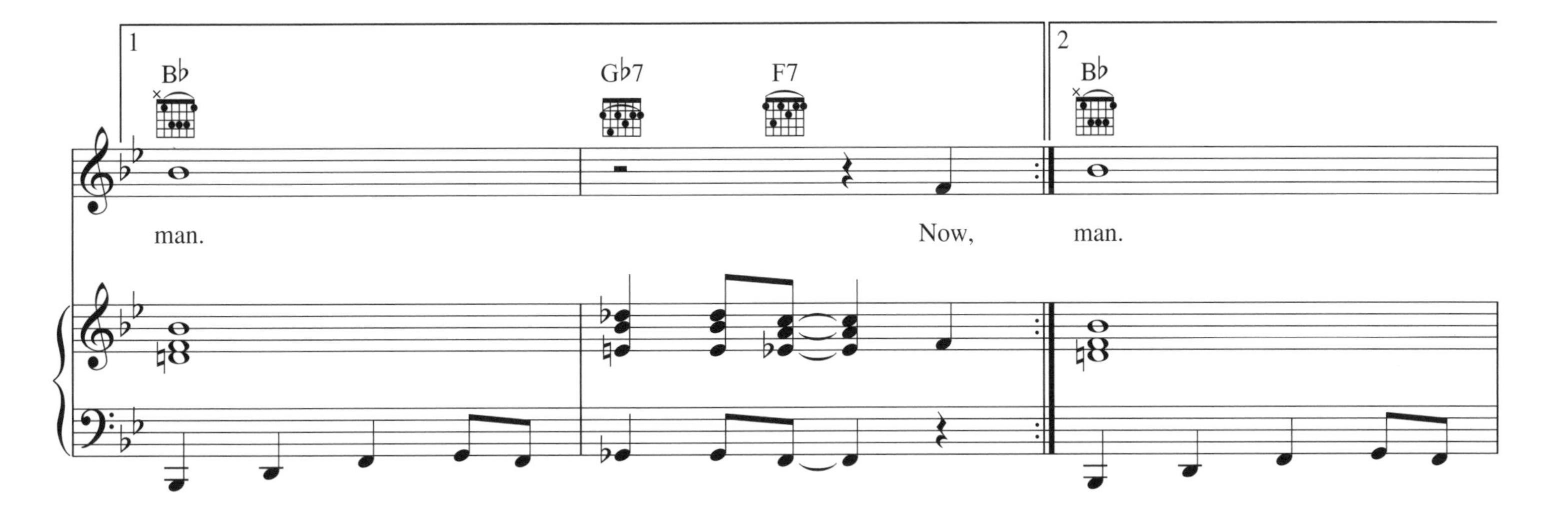
1
2
B♭
G♭7
F7
man.
Now,
man.

G♭7
F7
B♭
N.C.
Now,
Sam - son told De - li - lah loud and clear:
heard 'bout a king who was do - in' swell
I got a wom - an a head like a rock.

B♭
N.C.
E♭7
Keep your cot - ton - pick - in' fin - gers out my curl - y hair.
till he start - ed play - in' with that e - vil Jez - e - bel.
If she ev - er went a - way, I'd cry a - round the clock.
Oh, yeah,

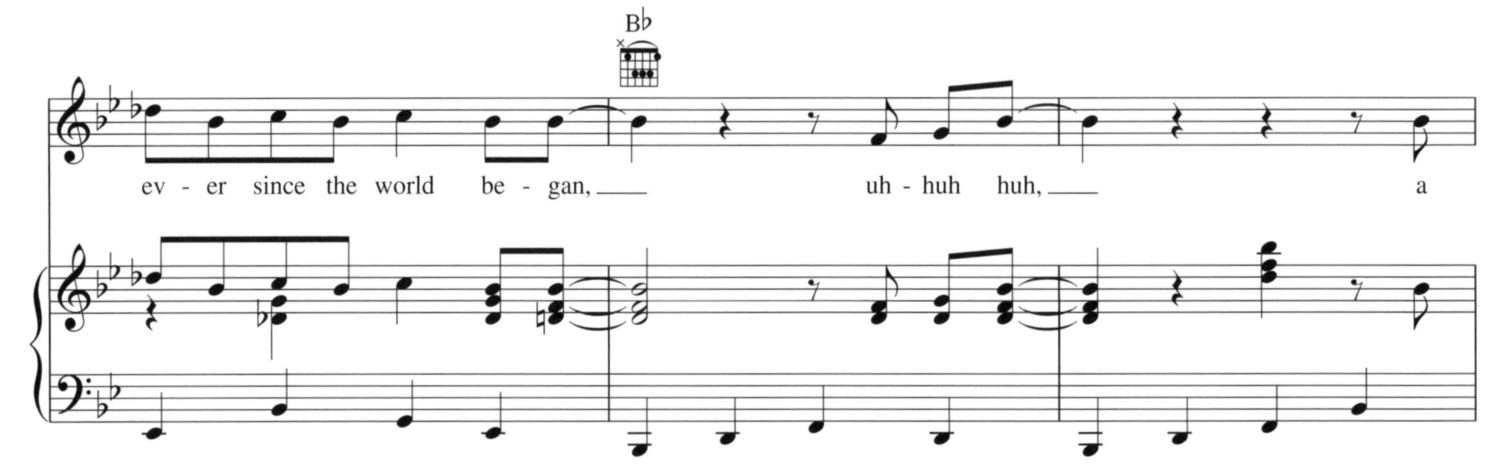
B♭
ev - er since the world be - gan, uh - huh huh, a

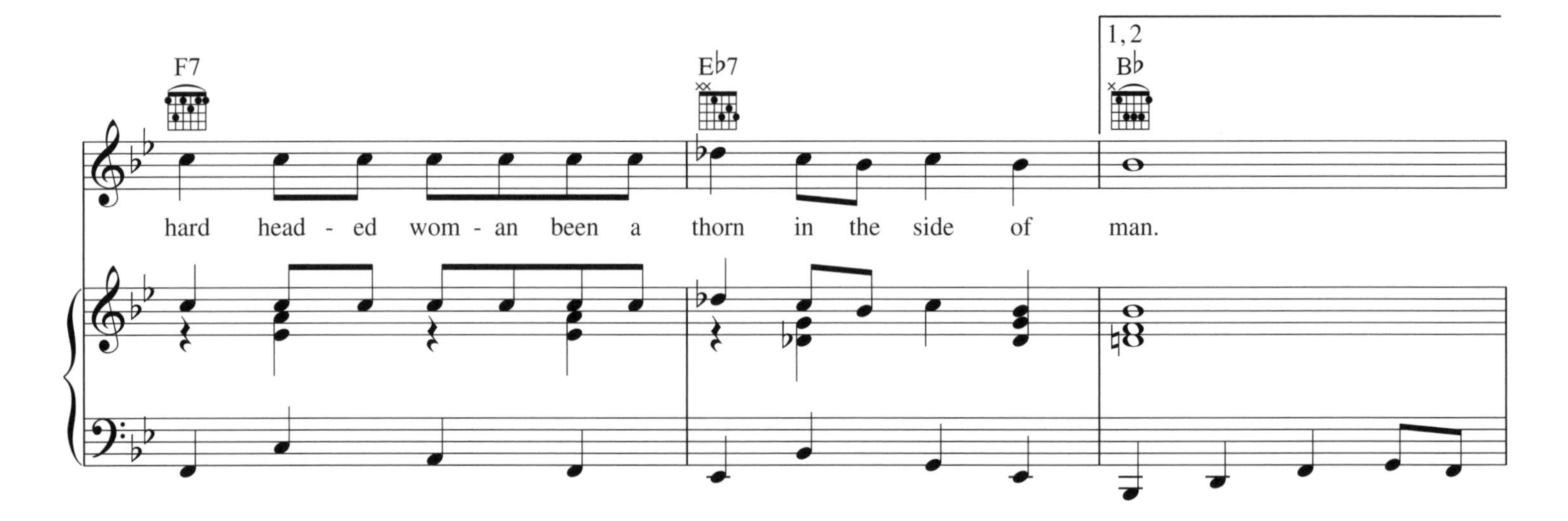
F7
E♭7
1, 2
B♭
hard head - ed wom - an been a thorn in the side of man.

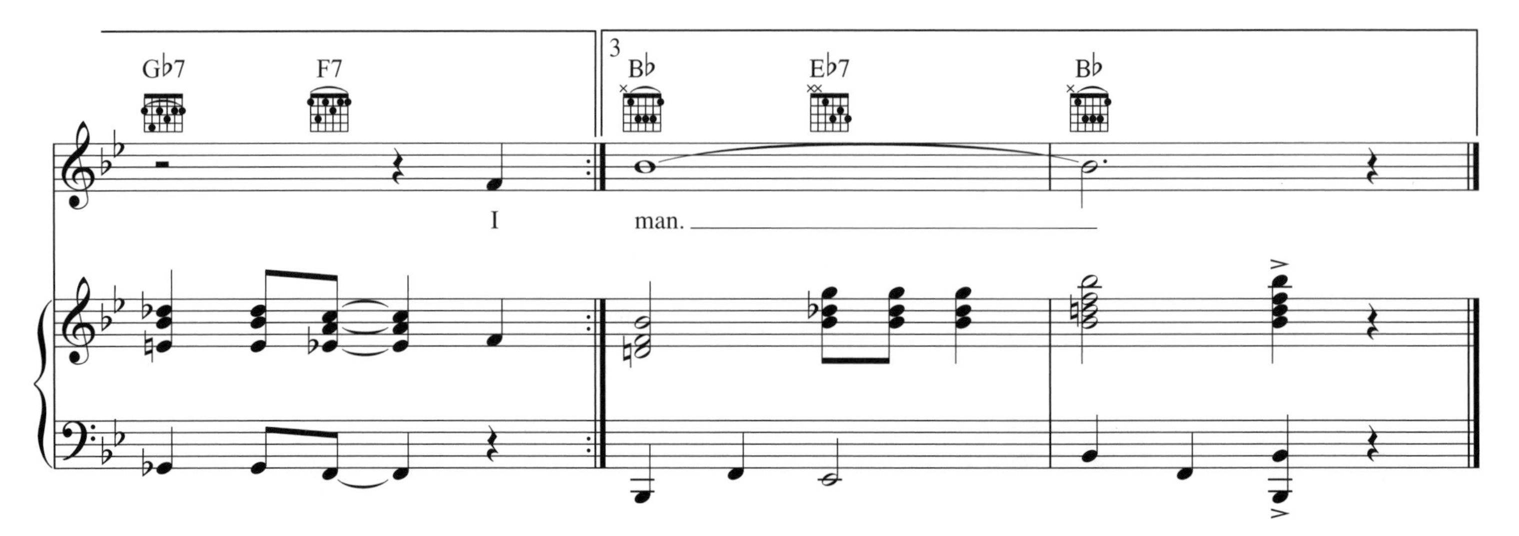
G♭7
F7
3
B♭
E♭7
B♭
I man.

GUITAR MAN

By JERRY REED

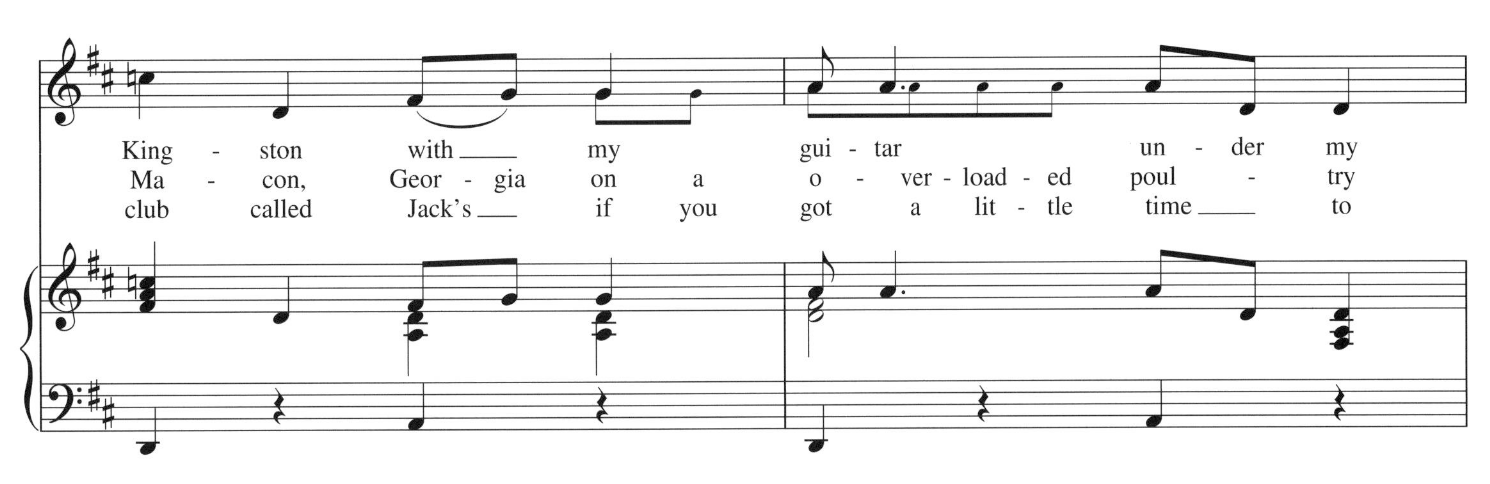

G7sus
G7
coat. I hitch-hiked all the way down to Mem-phis, got a room at the
truck. I thumbed on down to Pan - a - ma Cit - y, start - ed pick - in' out
kill. Just fol - low that crowd of peo - ple, you'll wind up
D7
Y. M. C. A. For the next three weeks I went a -
some of them all - night bars, hop - in' I can make my -
out on his dance floor, dig - gin' the fin - est lit - tle
haunt - ing them night - clubs, look - ing for a place to
self a dol - lar mak - in' mu - sic on my gui -
five - piece group up and down the Gulf of Mex - i -
A7
play. Well, I thought my pick - ing would
tar. Got the same old sto - ry at them
co. And guess who's lead - ing that

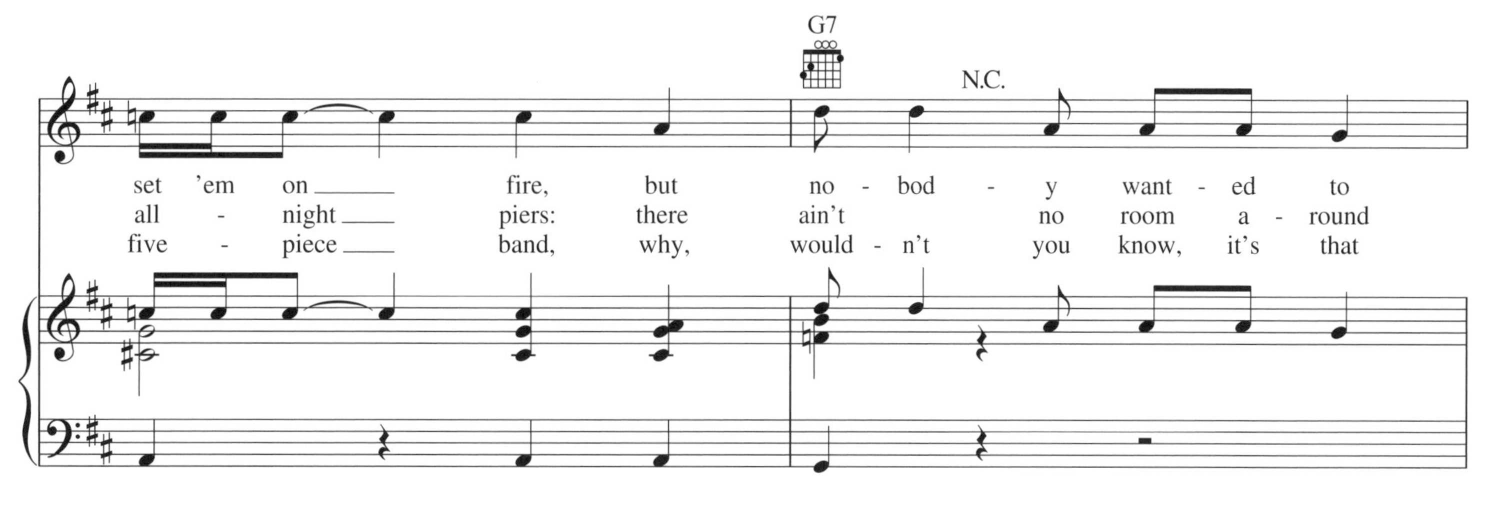
G7
N.C.
set 'em on fire, but no - bod - y want - ed to
all - night piers: there ain't no room a - round
five - piece band, why, would - n't you know, it's that

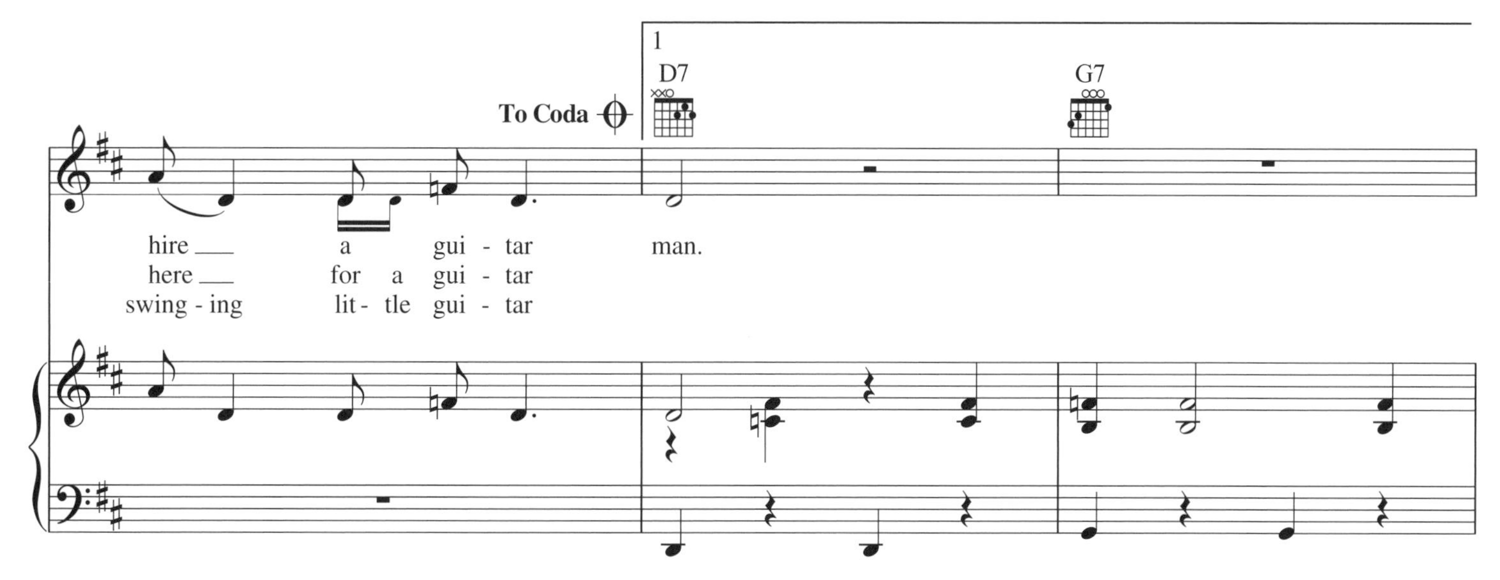
To Coda
1
D7
G7
hire a gui - tar man.
here for a gui - tar
swing - ing lit - tle gui - tar

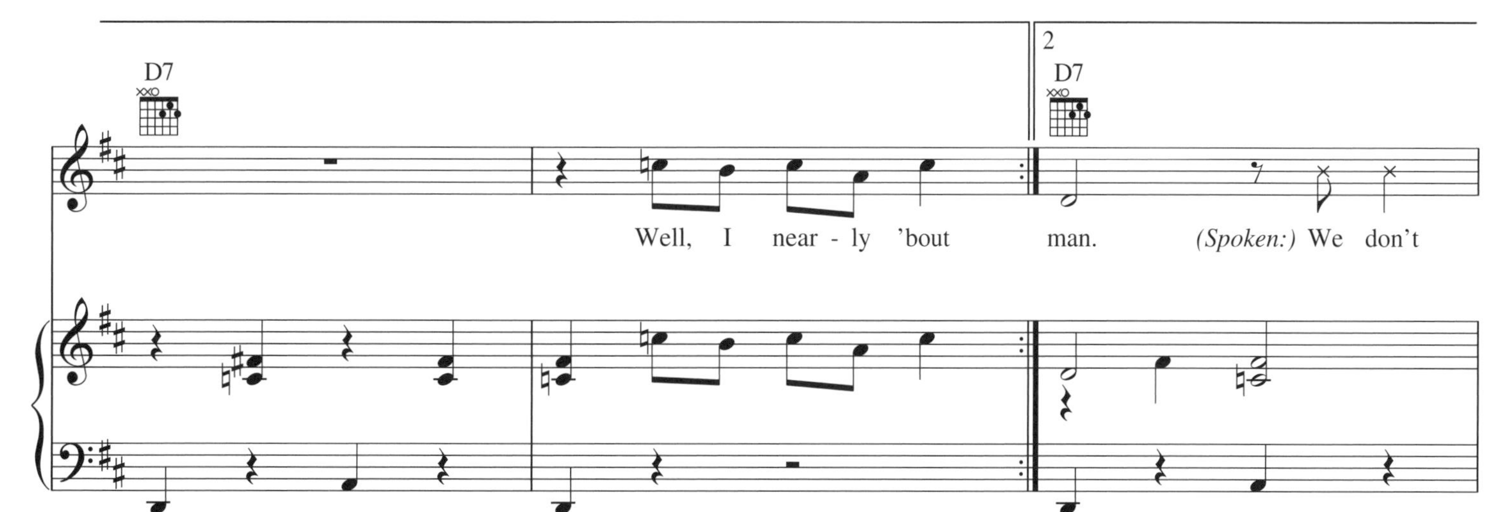
D7
2
D7
Well, I near - ly 'bout man. (Spoken:) We don't

need a gui - tar man, son. So I

G7
slept in the ho - bo jun - gles. I bummed a thou - sand miles of

D7
track 'til I found my - self in Mo - bile, Al - a - bam - a in a

G7
club they call "Big Jack's." A lit - tle four - piece band was

jam - ming, so I took my gui - tar and I sat in. I

E7
A7
showed 'em what a band would sound like with a swing - in' lit - tle gui - tar

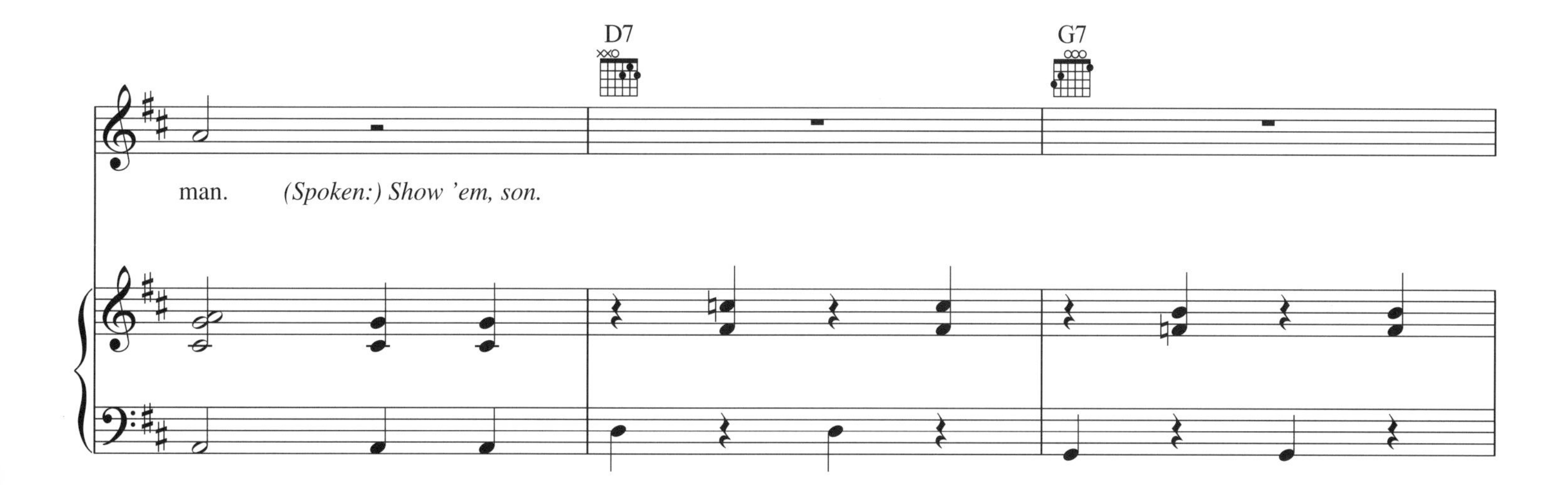
D7
G7
man. (Spoken:) Show 'em, son.

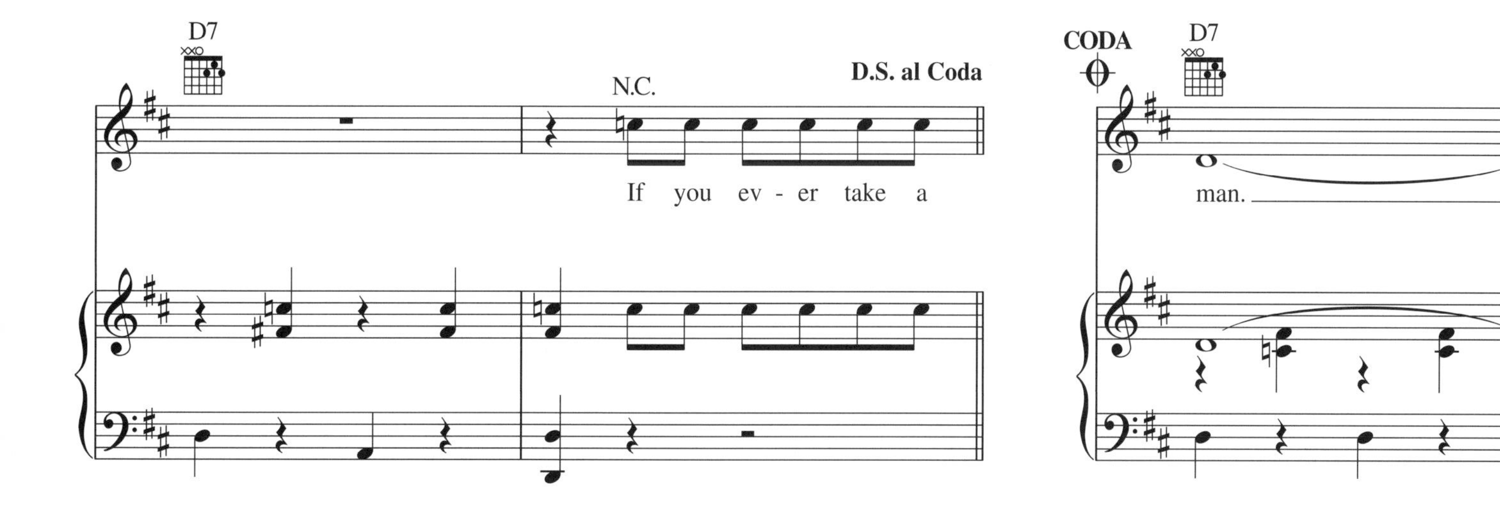
D7
N.C.
D.S. al Coda
If you ev - er take a
CODA
D7
man.

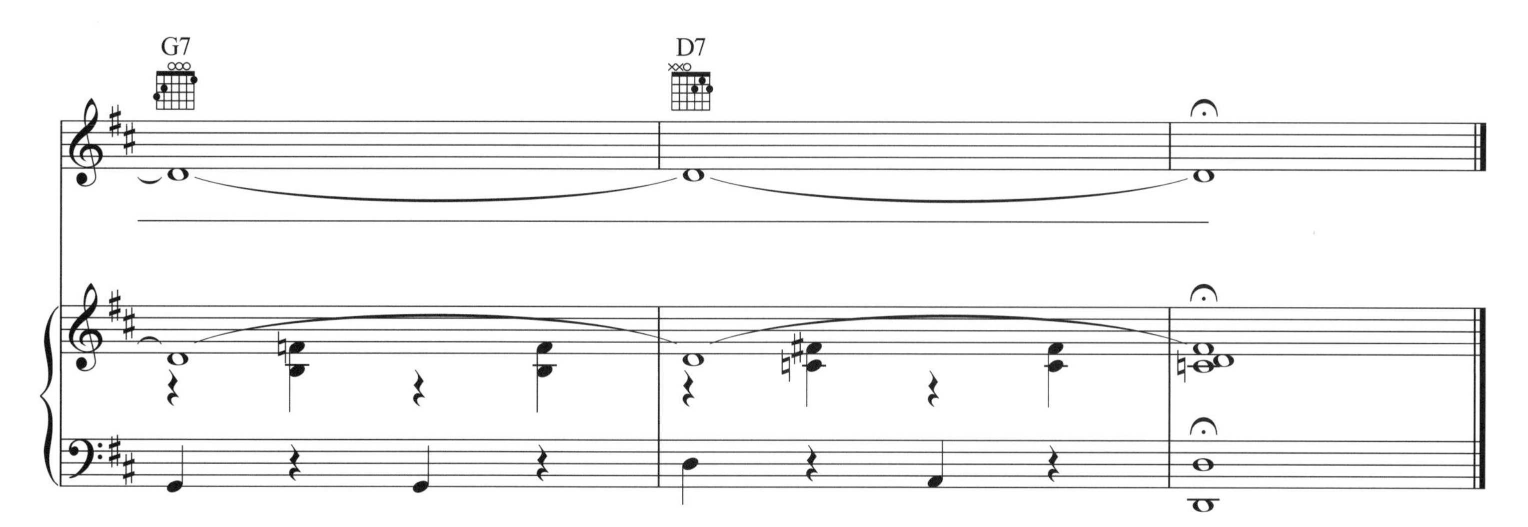
G7
D7

HEARTBREAK HOTEL

Words and Music by MAE BOREN AXTON,
TOMMY DURDEN and ELVIS PRESLEY

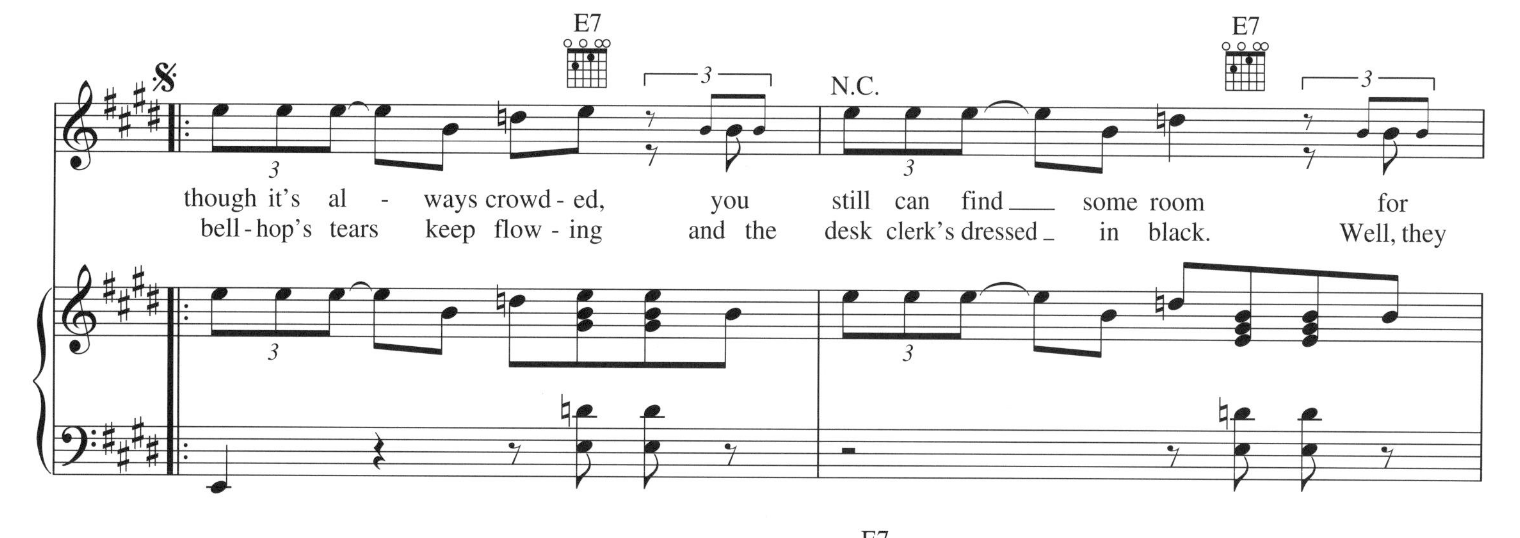
E7
N.C.
E7
though it's al - ways crowd - ed, you still can find some room for
bell - hop's tears keep flow - ing and the desk clerk's dressed in black. Well, they

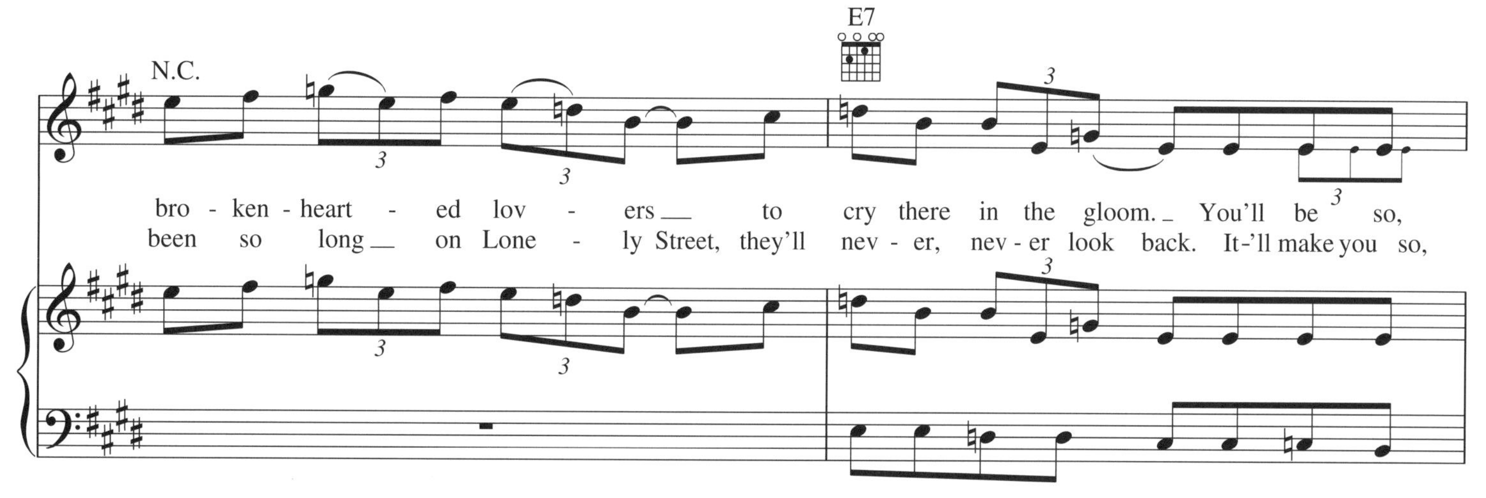
N.C.
E7
bro - ken - heart - ed lov - ers to cry there in the gloom. You'll be so,
been so long on Lone - ly Street, they'll nev - er, nev - er look back. It-'ll make you so,

A7
it - 'll make you so lone - ly, ba - by. It - 'll make you so lone - ly.
it - 'll make you so lone - ly, ba - by. Well, they're so lone - ly.
B7
To Coda
1
E
2
E
Oh, they're so lone - ly they could die. Now, the die. Well, now
Oh, they're so lone - ly they could

E7
N.C.
E7
if your ba - by leaves you and you've got a tale to tell, well, just
Instrumental solo
N.C.
E7
A7
take a walk down Lone-ly Street to Heart-break Ho-tel where you will be, you will be so lone - ly, ba - by.
B7
1
E
Well, you'll be lone - ly. You'll be so lone - ly you could die.
2
E
D.S. al Coda
(Verse 2)
Solo ends Al -
CODA
E
F7
E7
die.

HOUND DOG

Words and Music by JERRY LEIBER
and MIKE STOLLER

G7
F7
C
never caught a rabbit and you ain't no friend of mine.
N.C.
C
Well, they said you was high - classed,
but, that was just a
lie.
F7
Yeah, they said you was high - classed,
C
but, that was just a lie.
Yeah, you ain't

G7
F7
C
nev - er caught a rab - bit and you ain't no friend of mine.

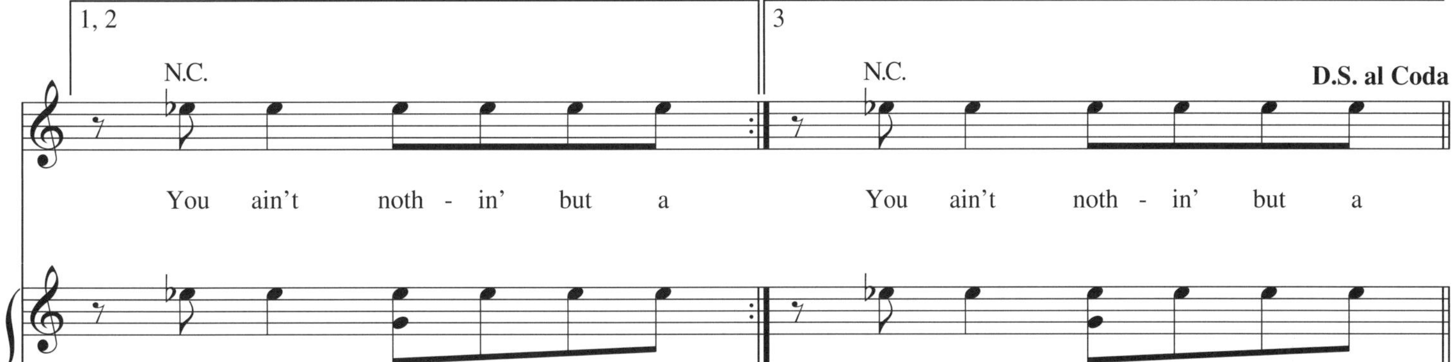
1, 2
N.C.
You ain't noth - in' but a
3
N.C.
D.S. al Coda
You ain't noth - in' but a

CODA
G7
F7
nev - er caught a rab - bit, and you ain't no friend of mine.

C
C7

I BEG OF YOU

Words and Music by ROSE MARIE McCOY
and KELLY OWENS

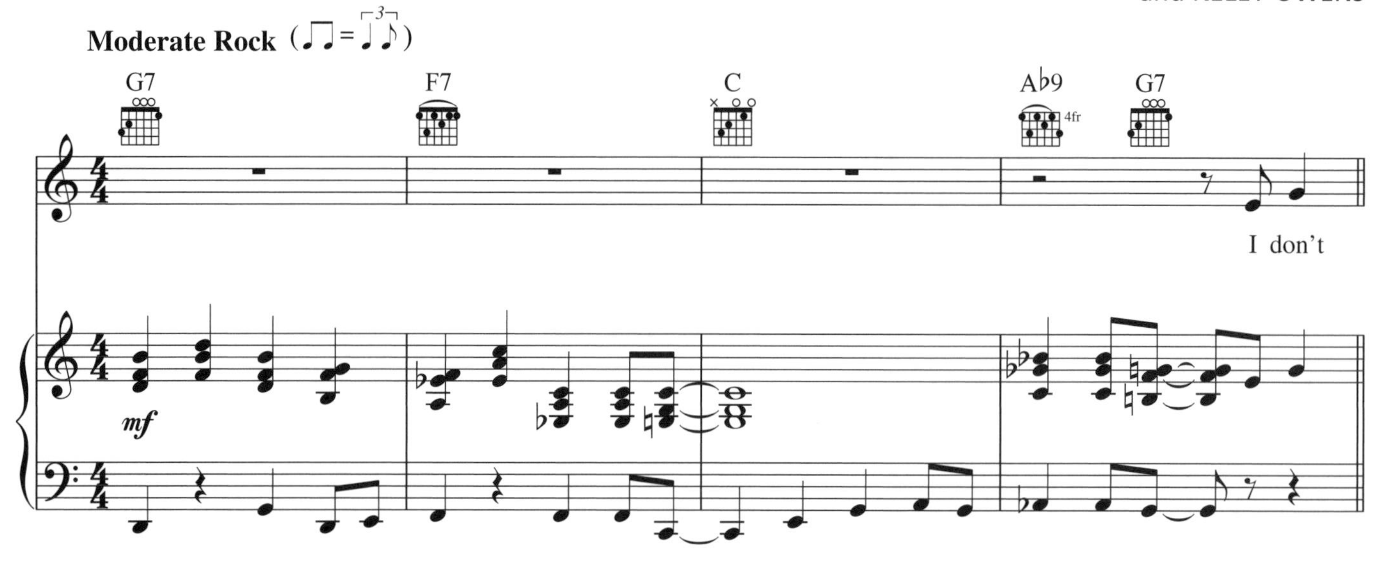

C
G7
know I care a lot. Dar - ling, please don't break my
ev - er say good - bye. Dar - ling, please don't say good -

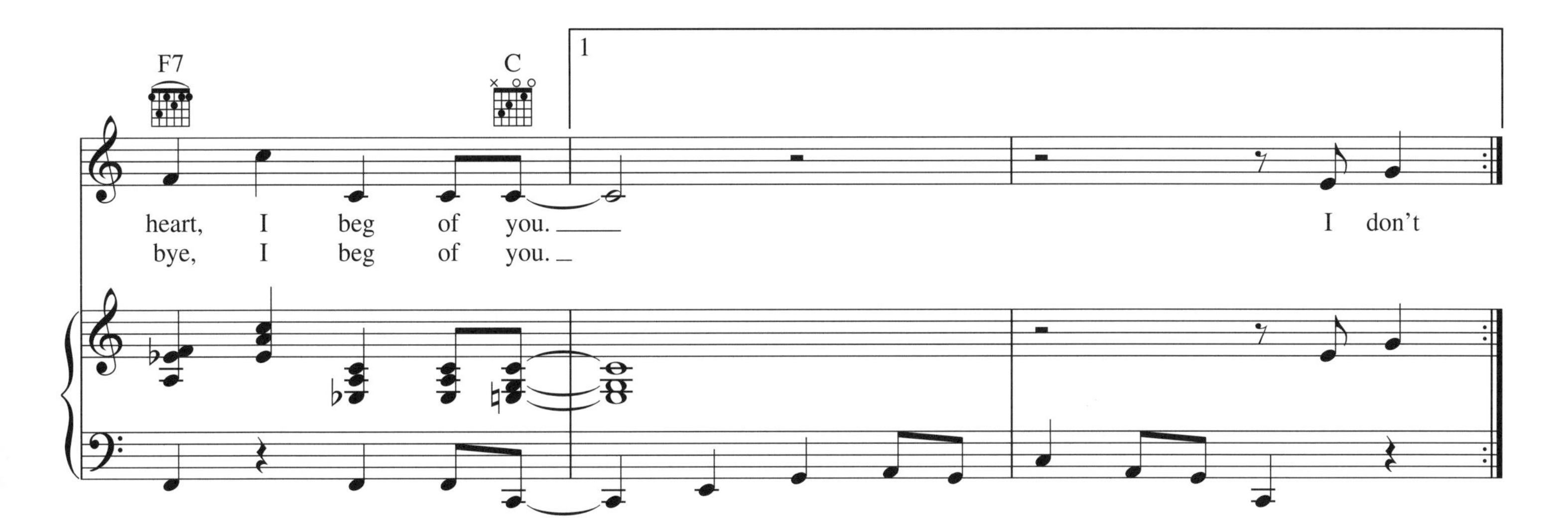
F7
C
1
heart, I beg of you. I don't
bye, I beg of you.

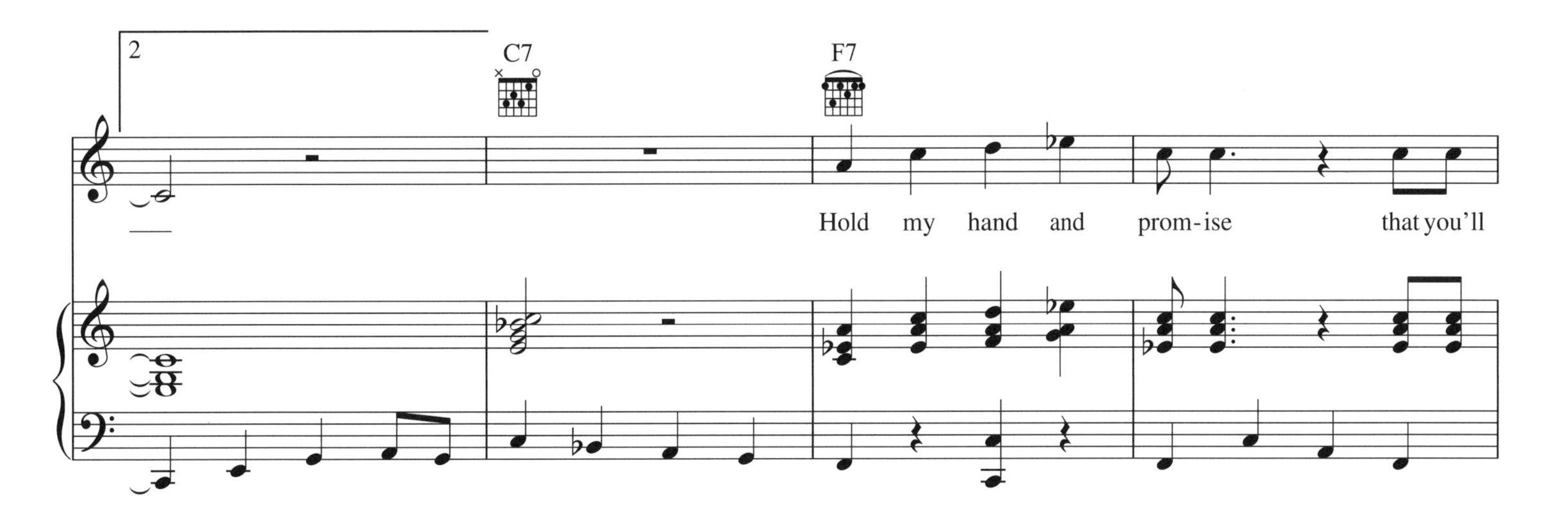
2
C7
F7
Hold my hand and prom - ise that you'll

C
F7
al - ways love me true. Make me know you love me the

D7
N.C.
F/G
C
same way I love you, lit - tle girl. You got me at your mer - cy now

C7
F7
that I'm in love with you. So, please don't take ad -

C
van - tage 'cause you know my love is true. My dar - ling,

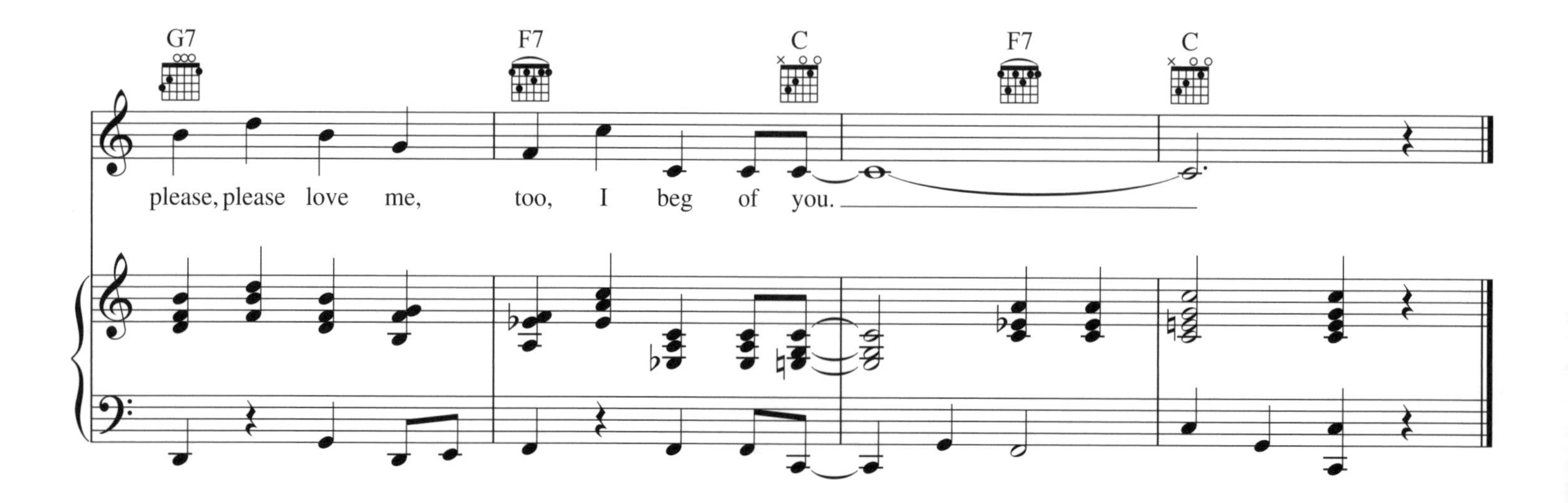
G7
F7
C
F7
C
please, please love me, too, I beg of you.

I FORGOT TO REMEMBER TO FORGET

Words and Music by STANLEY A. KESLER
and CHARLIE FEATHERS

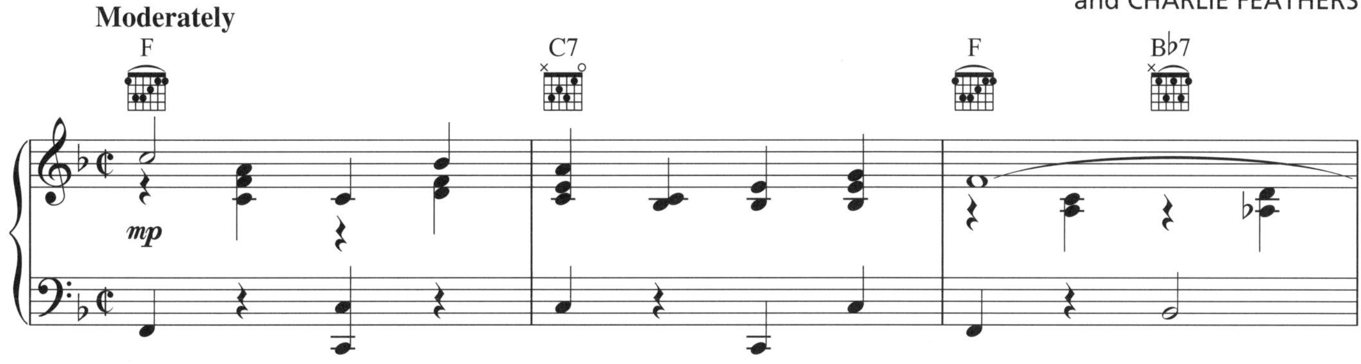

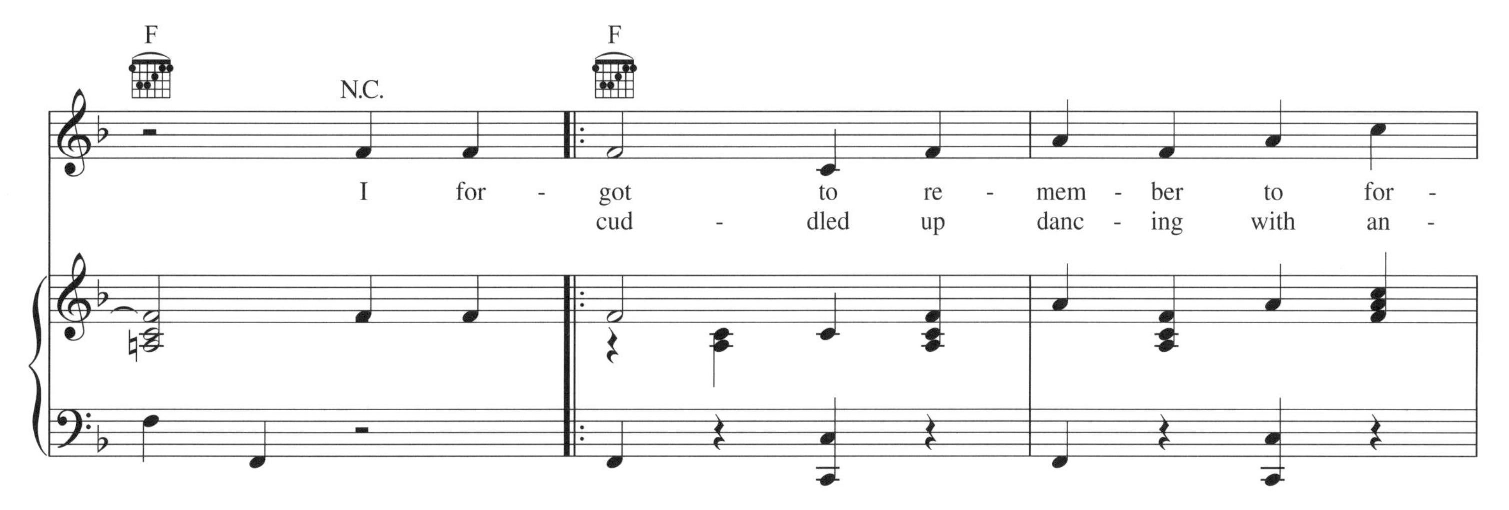

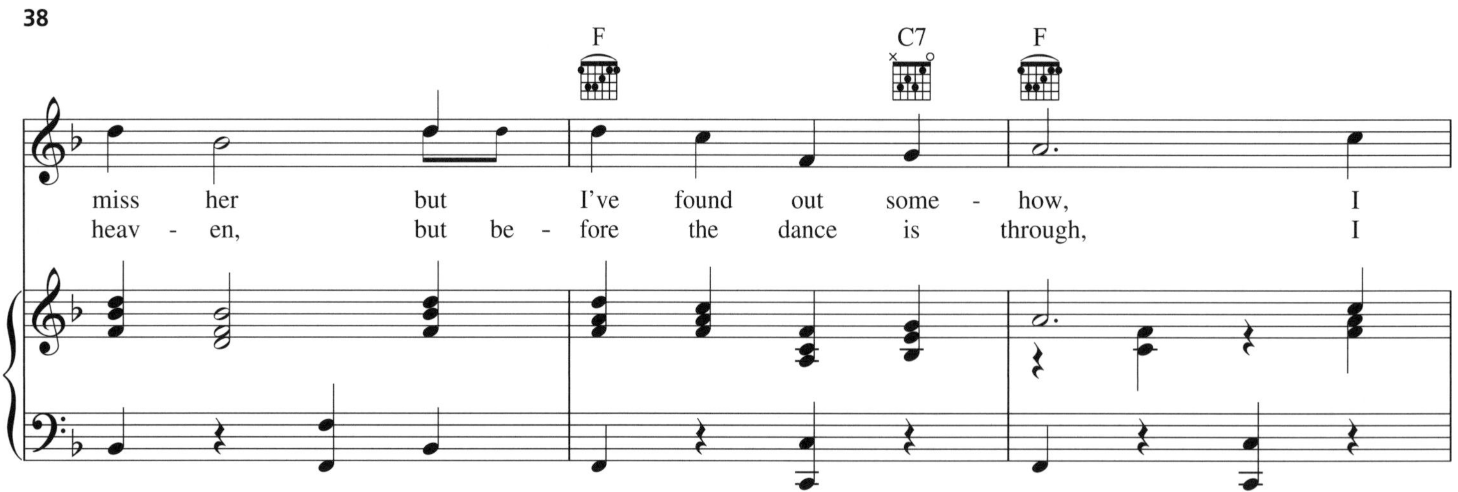
F
C7
F
miss her but I've found out some - how, I
heav - en, but be - fore the dance is through, I

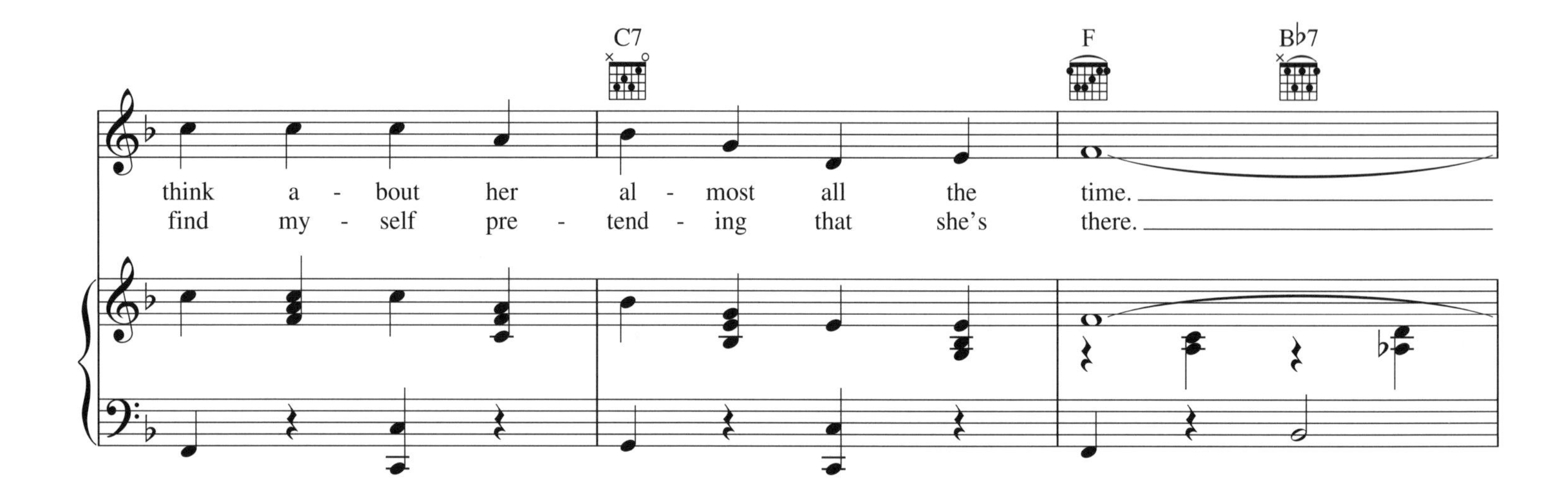
C7
F
B♭7
think a - bout her al - most all the time.
find my - self pre - tend - ing that she's there.

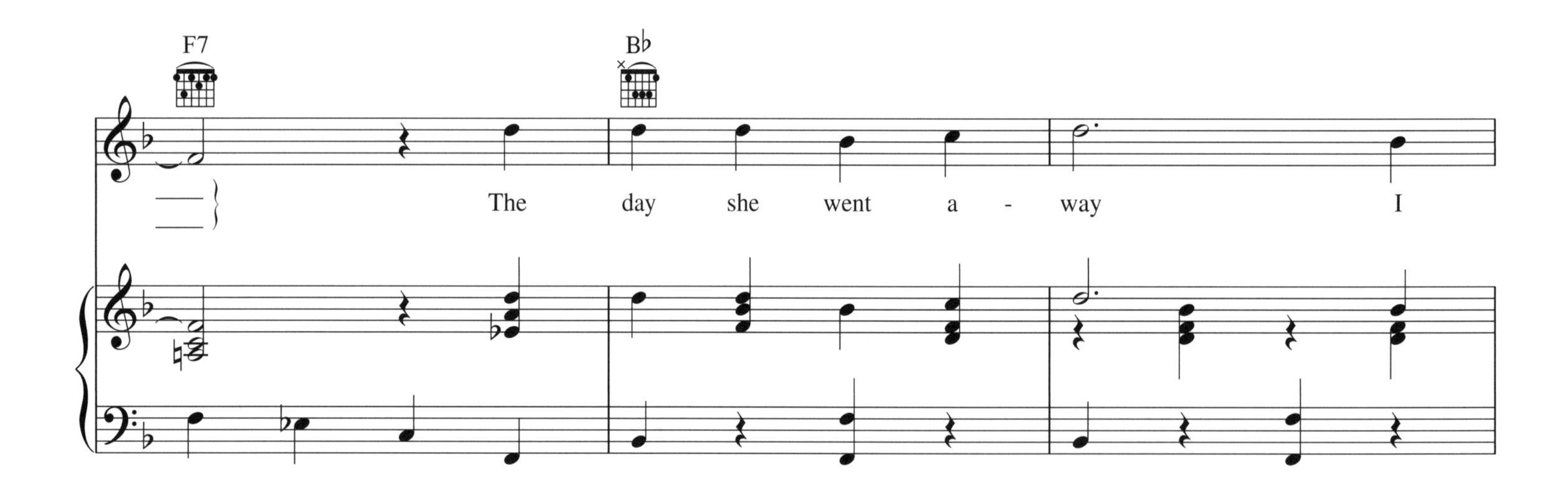
F7
B♭
The day she went a - way I

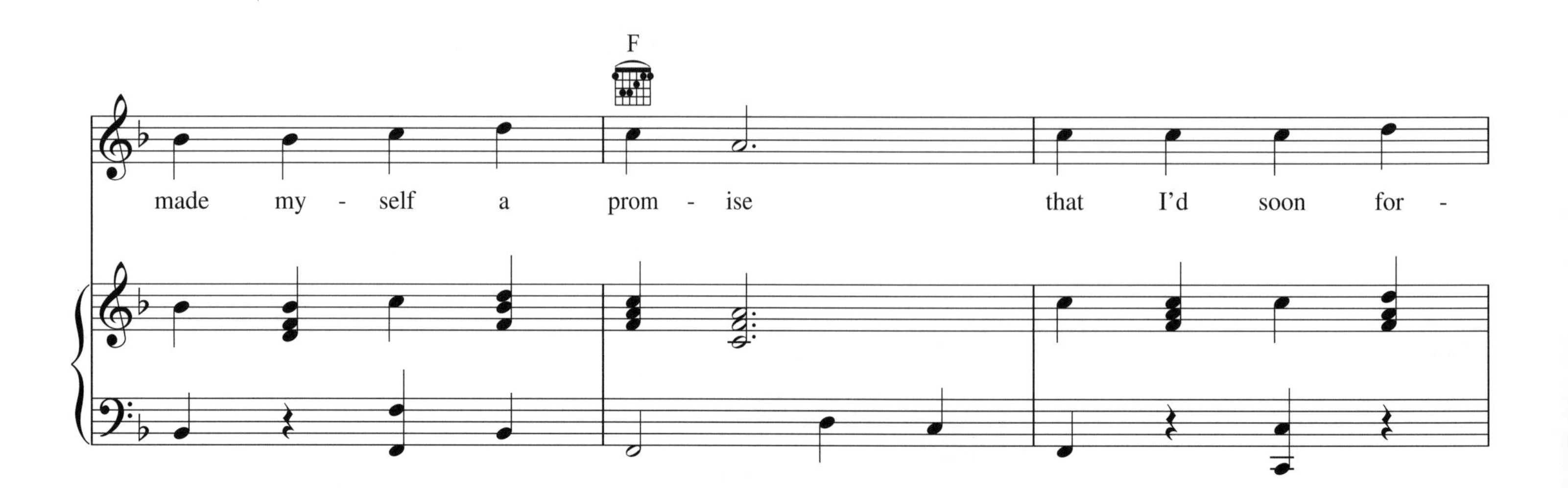
F
made my - self a prom - ise that I'd soon for -

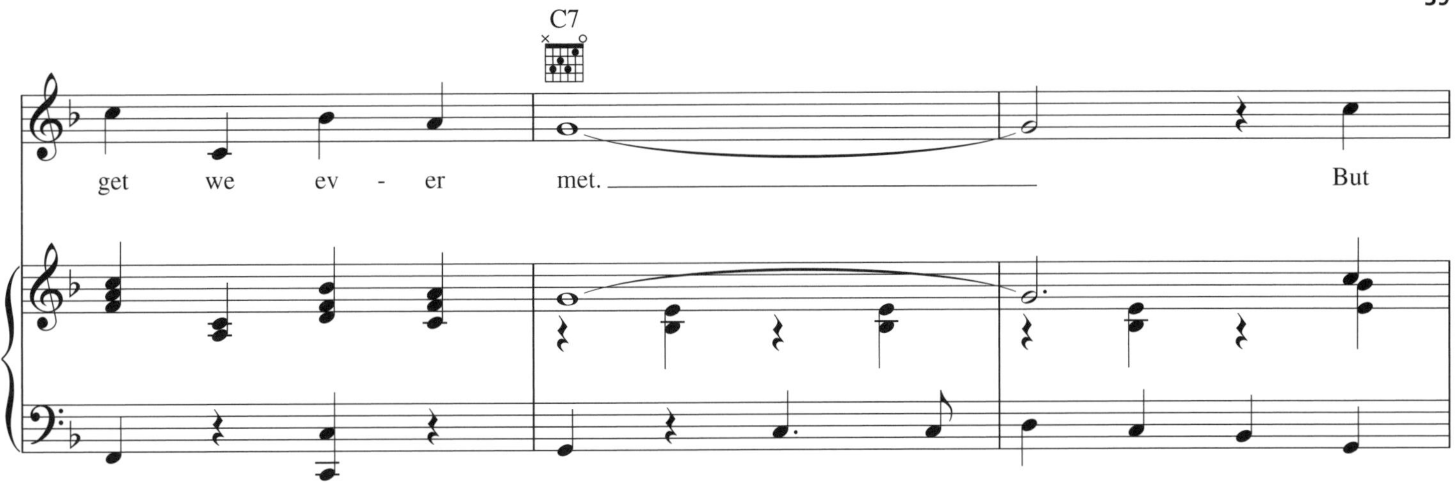
C7
get we ev - er met. But

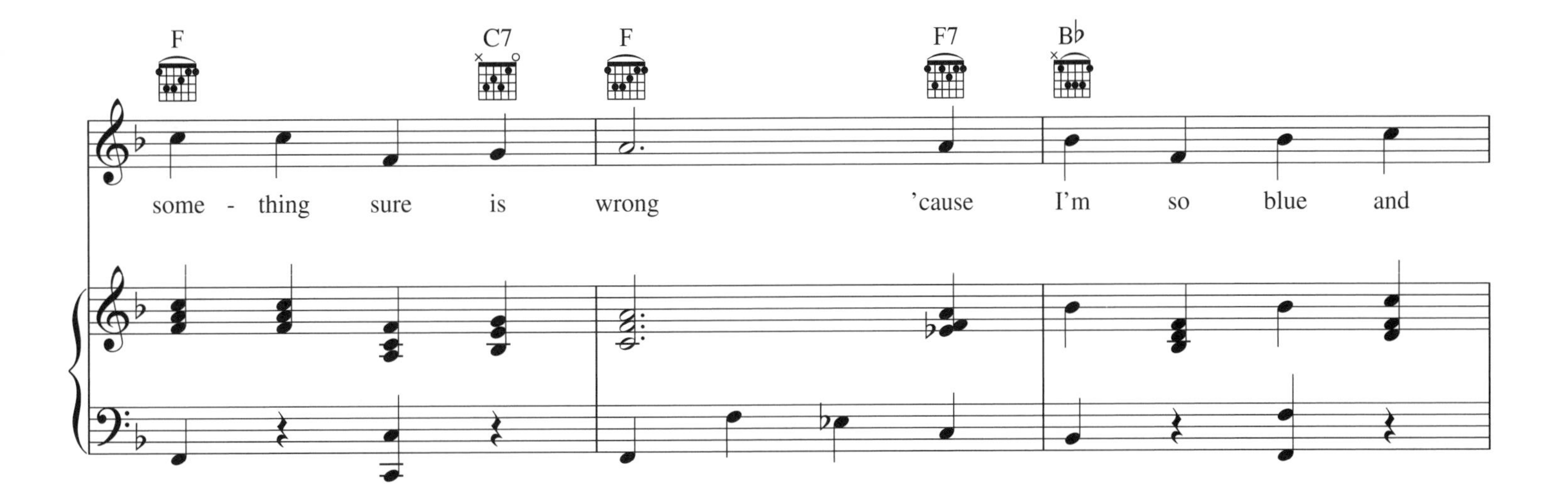
F C7 F F7 B♭
some - thing sure is wrong 'cause I'm so blue and

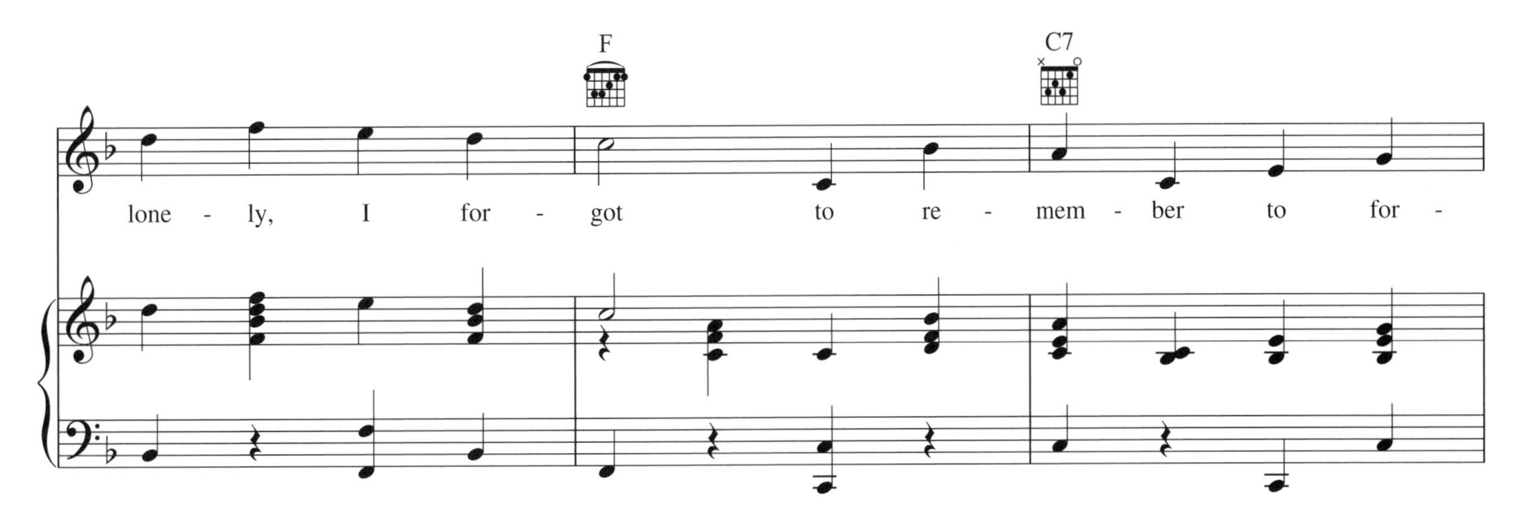
F C7
lone - ly, I for - got to re - mem - ber to for -

1 F B♭7 F N.C.
get. When I'm
2 F B♭7 F
get.

I WANT YOU, I NEED YOU, I LOVE YOU

Words and Music by MAURICE MYSELS
and IRA KOSLOFF

C
Am
Dm
G7
C
C7
time that you're near all my cares dis - ap - pear. Dar - ling, you're all that I'm liv - ing
F
C
E7
A7
for. I want you, I need you, I love you
Dm7
G7
C
Fm
C
Gm7
C7
more and more. I thought I could live with - out
F
Gm7
C7sus
C7
F
ro - mance, be - fore you came to me. But

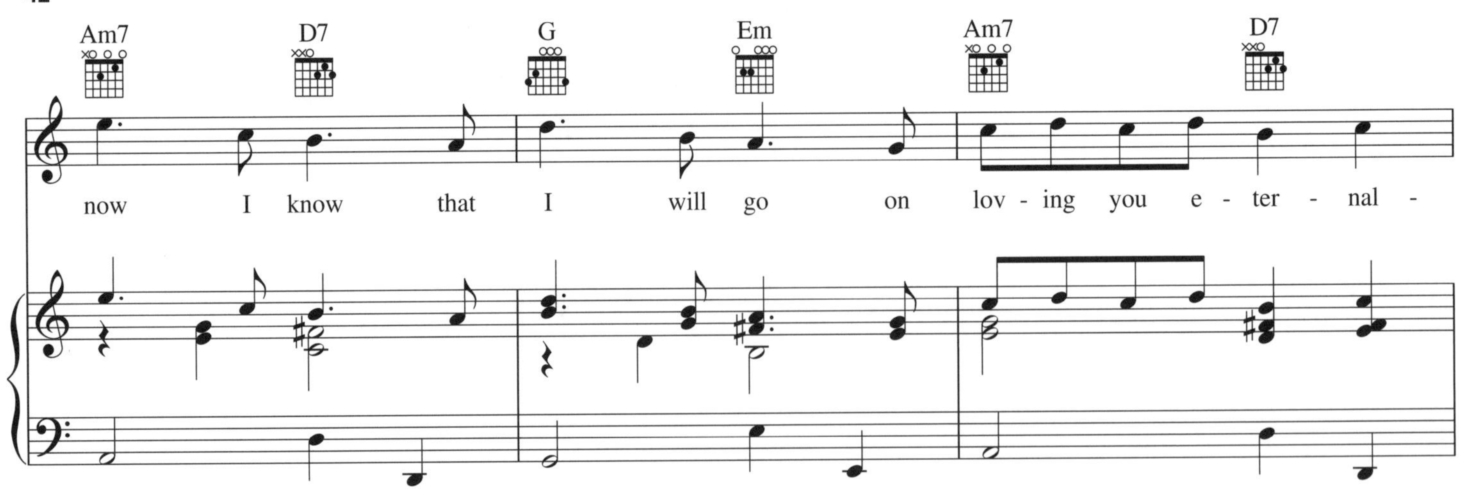
Am7 D7 G Em Am7 D7
now I know that I will go on lov - ing you e - ter - nal -

G7sus G7 C Am Dm G7
3
ly. Won't you please be my own? Nev - er leave me a - lone, 'cause I

C C7 F C E7
3
die ev - 'ry time we're a - part. I want you, I need you, I

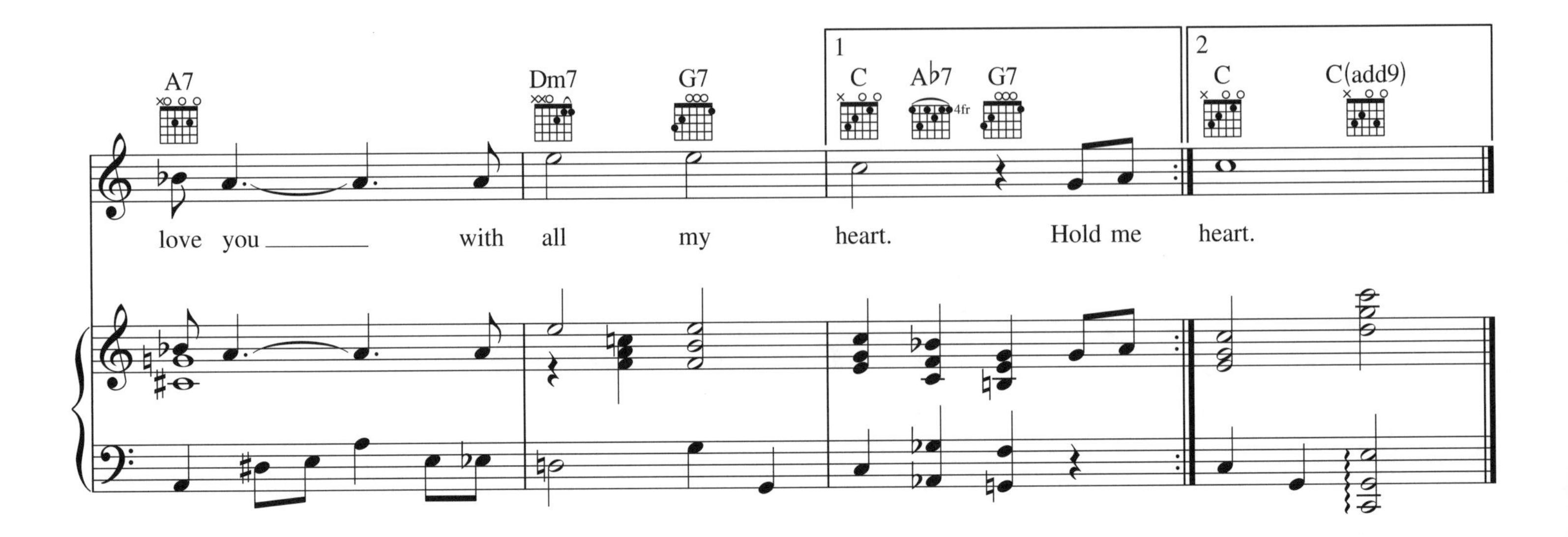
A7 Dm7 G7
1 C A♭7 G7
4fr
2 C C(add9)
love you with all my heart. Hold me heart.

I'VE GOT A THING ABOUT YOU, BABY

Words and Music by
TONY JOE WHITE

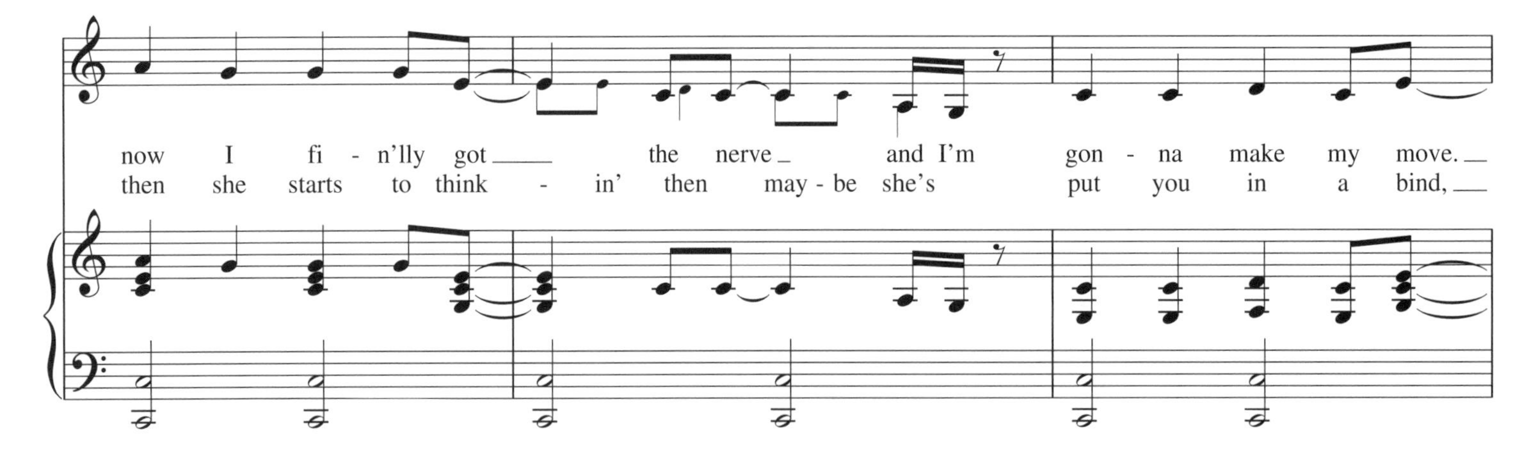
now I fi - n'lly got the nerve and I'm gon - na make my move.
then she starts to think - in' then may - be she's put you in a bind,

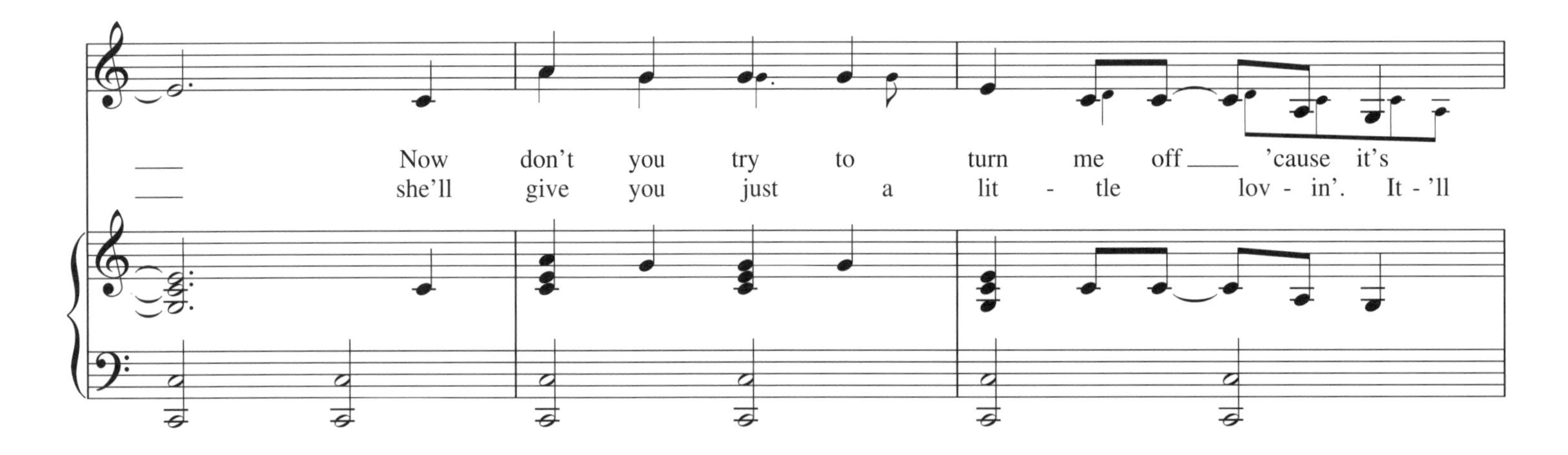
Now don't you try to turn me off 'cause it's
she'll give you just a lit - tle lov - in'. It - 'll

F
gon - na be here to do.
drive you out of your mind.
I got a thing a - bout you, ba -

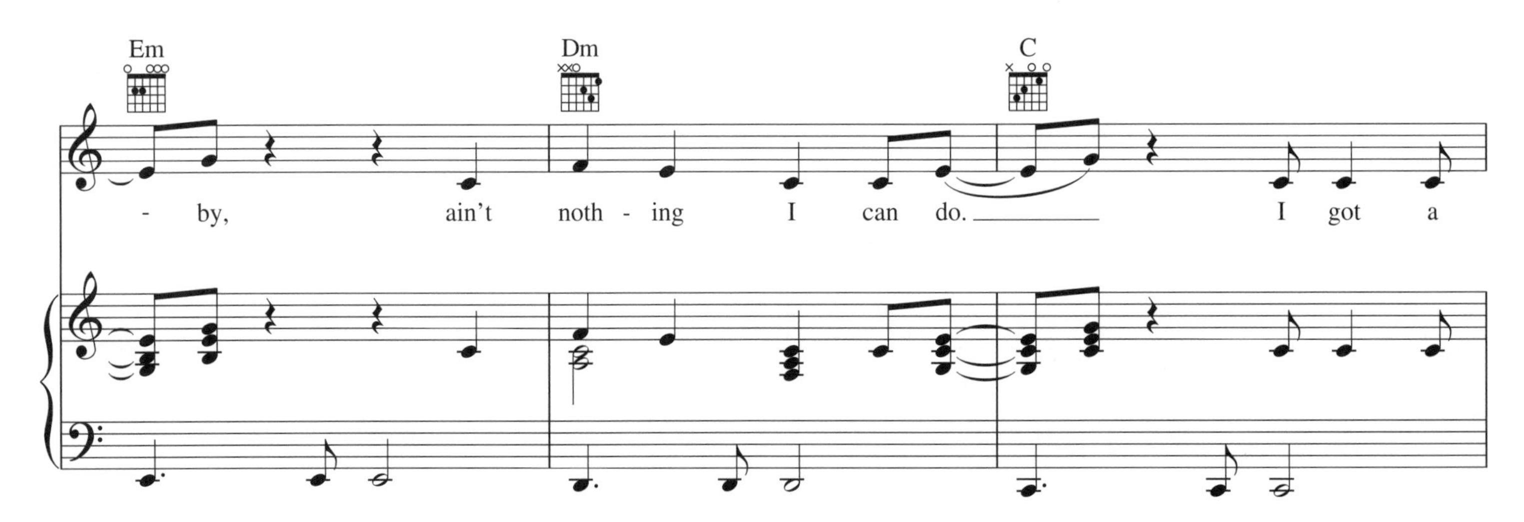
Em
Dm
C
- by, ain't noth - ing I can do. I got a

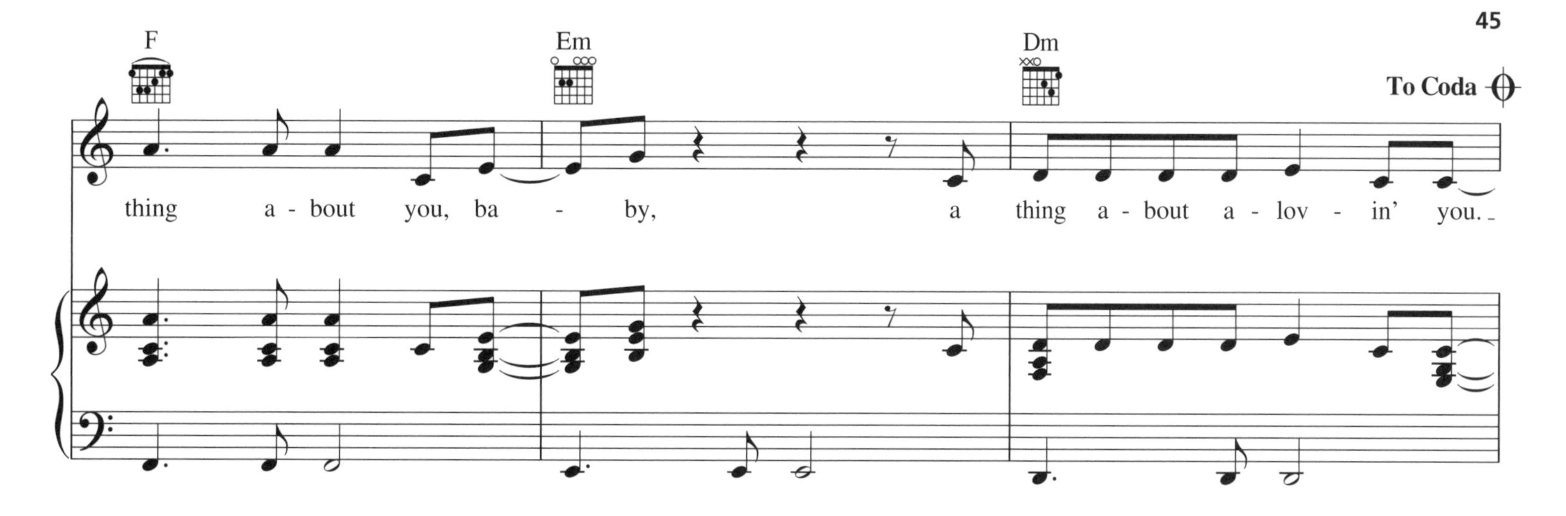
F
Em
Dm
To Coda
thing a - bout you, ba - by, a thing a - bout a - lov - in' you.

1
C
N.C.

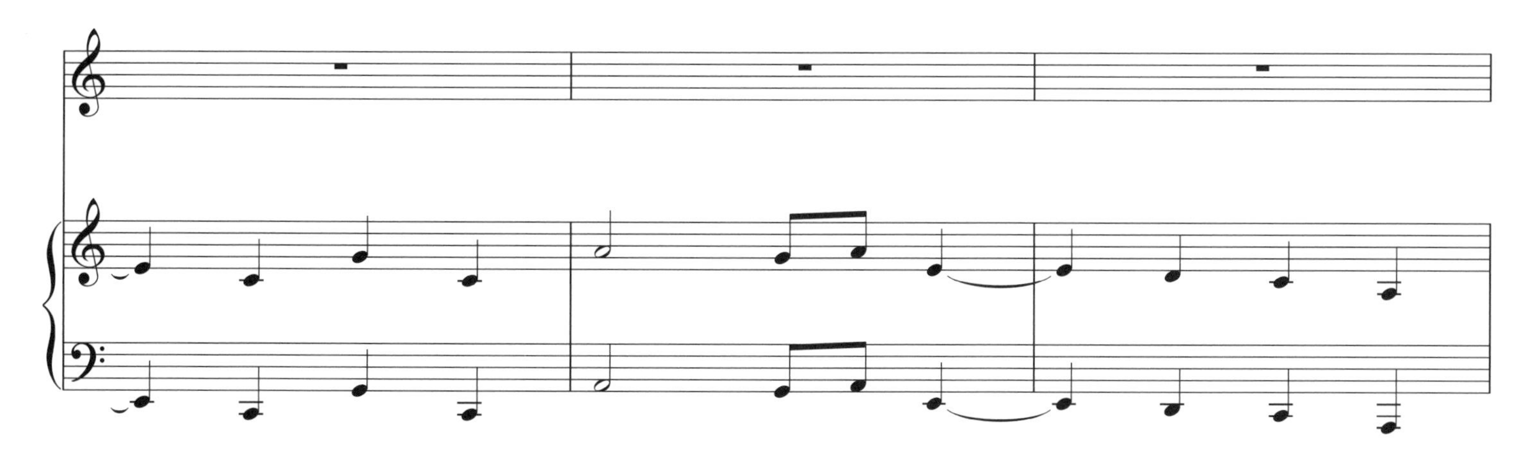

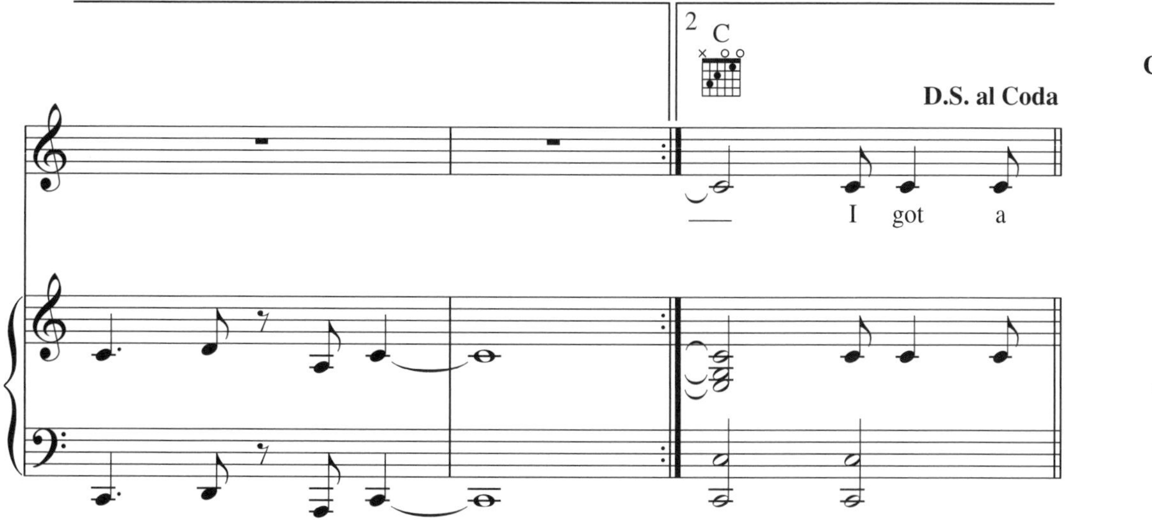
2
C
D.S. al Coda
I got a

CODA
C

I'M LEAVIN'

Words and Music by MICHAEL JARRETT
and SONNY CHARLES

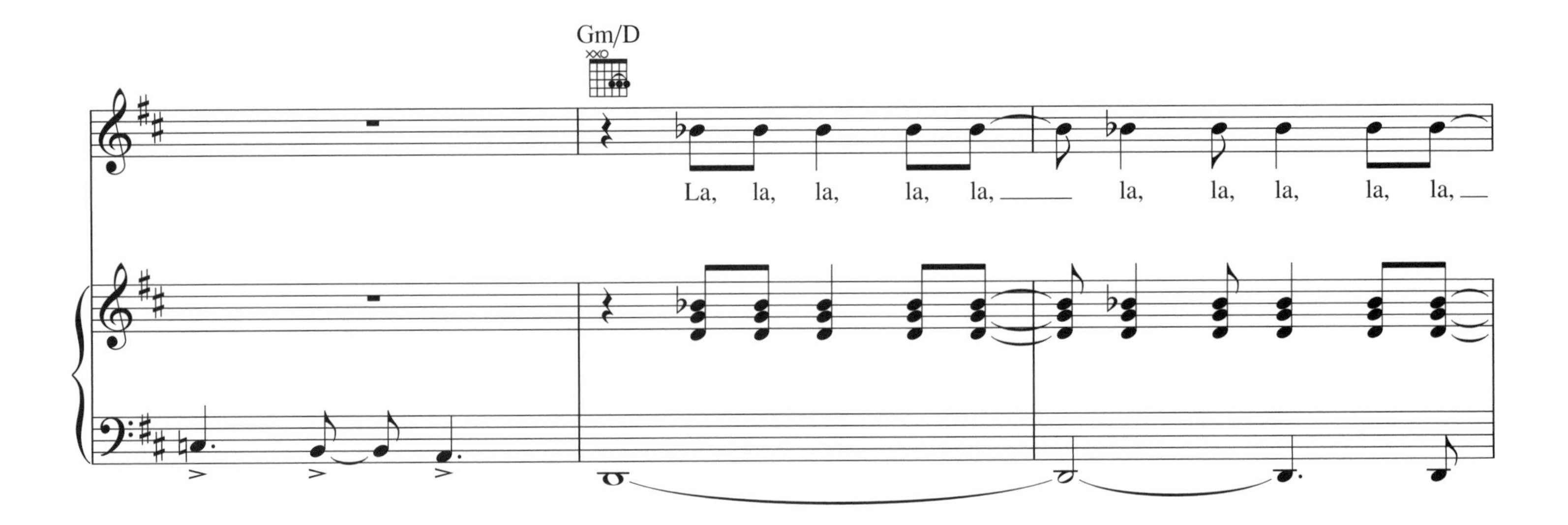

Dmaj7
D7
if I ar - rive in time to
Who will I have to lie be -

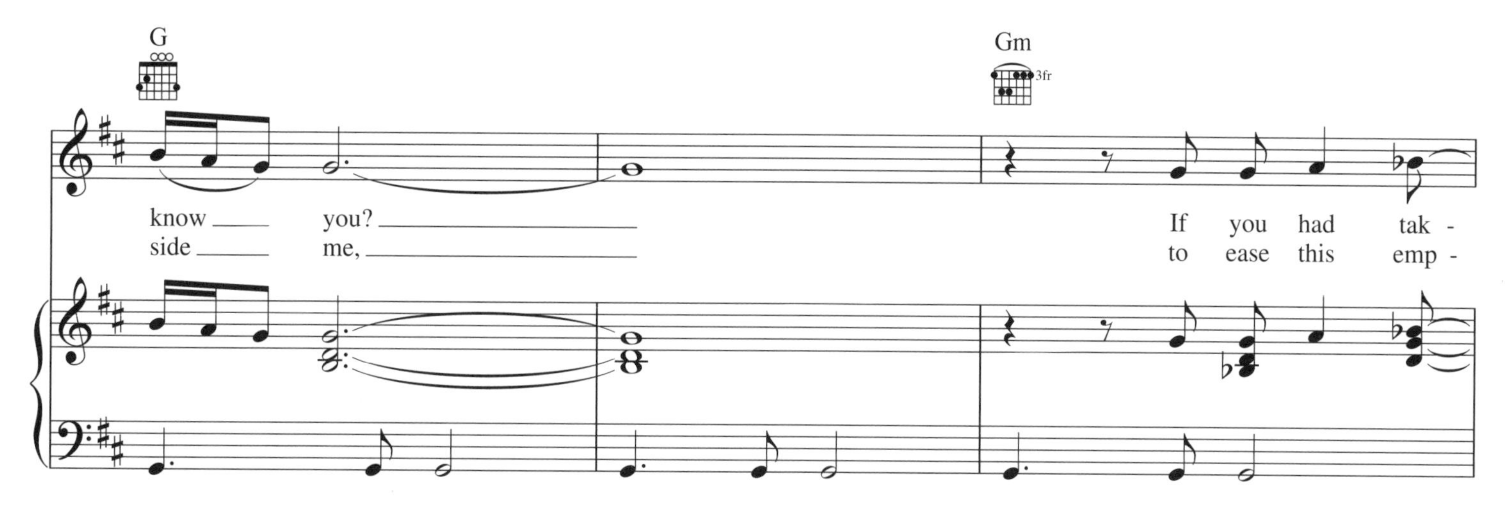
G
Gm
3fr
know you?
side me,
If you had tak -
to ease this emp -

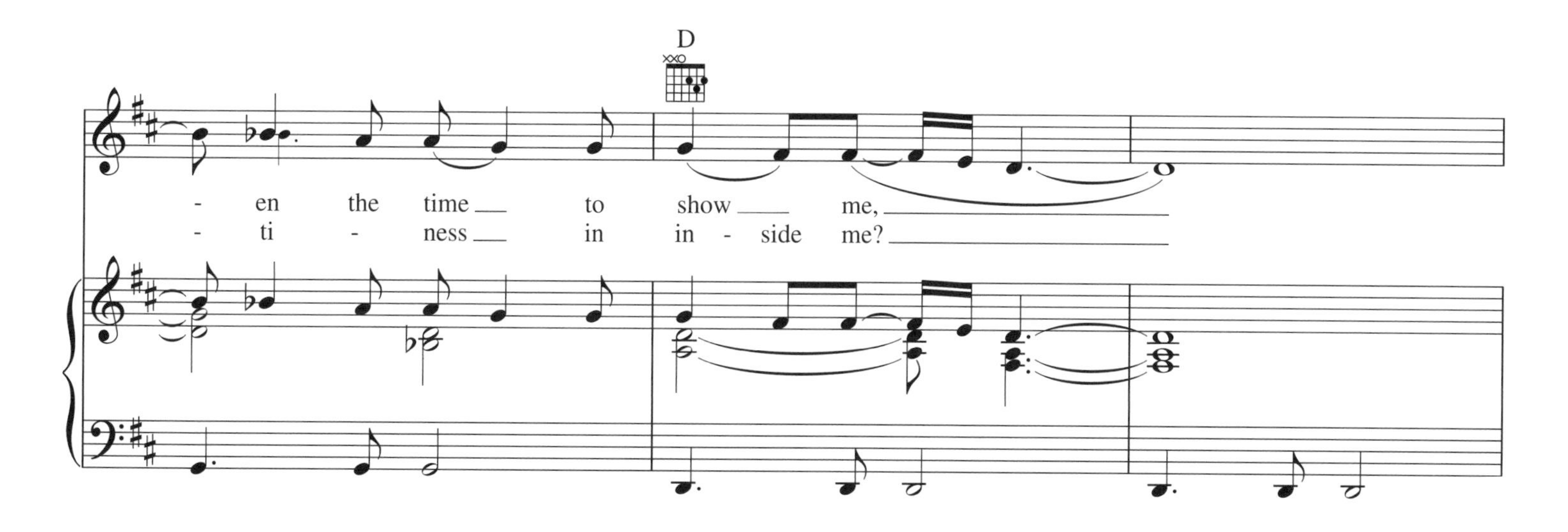
D
- en the time to show me,
- ti - ness in in - side me?

Em
F♯m
G
A
A7
I
I'm
would - n't be lone -
so lone -

1
D
2
D
- ly.
- ly.

A7
Tried so hard each time, each time I just can't make it.
mf

Feel - in' fast vi - bra - tions, and I just can't take it.

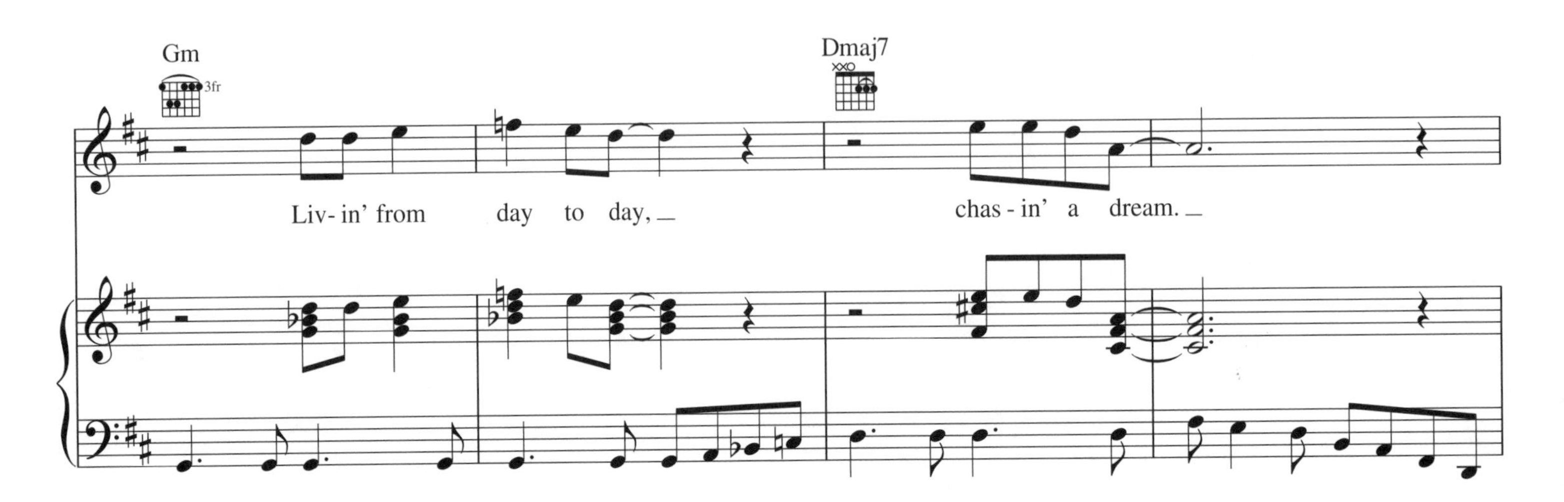
Gm
3fr
Dmaj7
Liv - in' from day to day, chas - in' a dream.

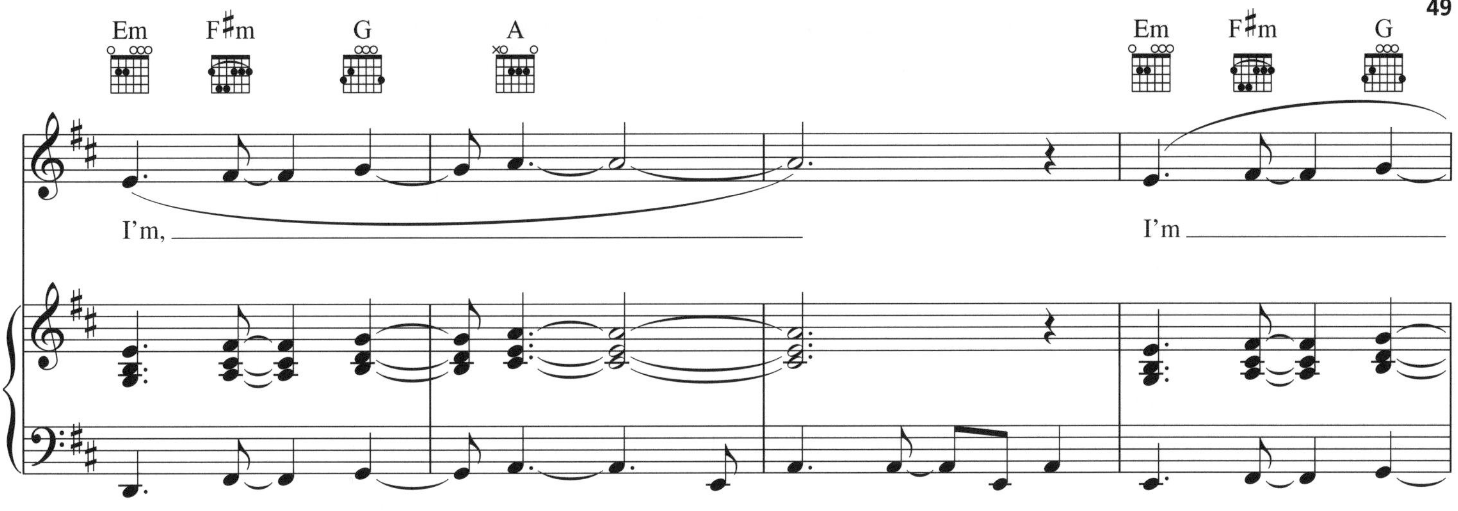
Em
F♯m
G
A
Em
F♯m
G
I'm,
I'm

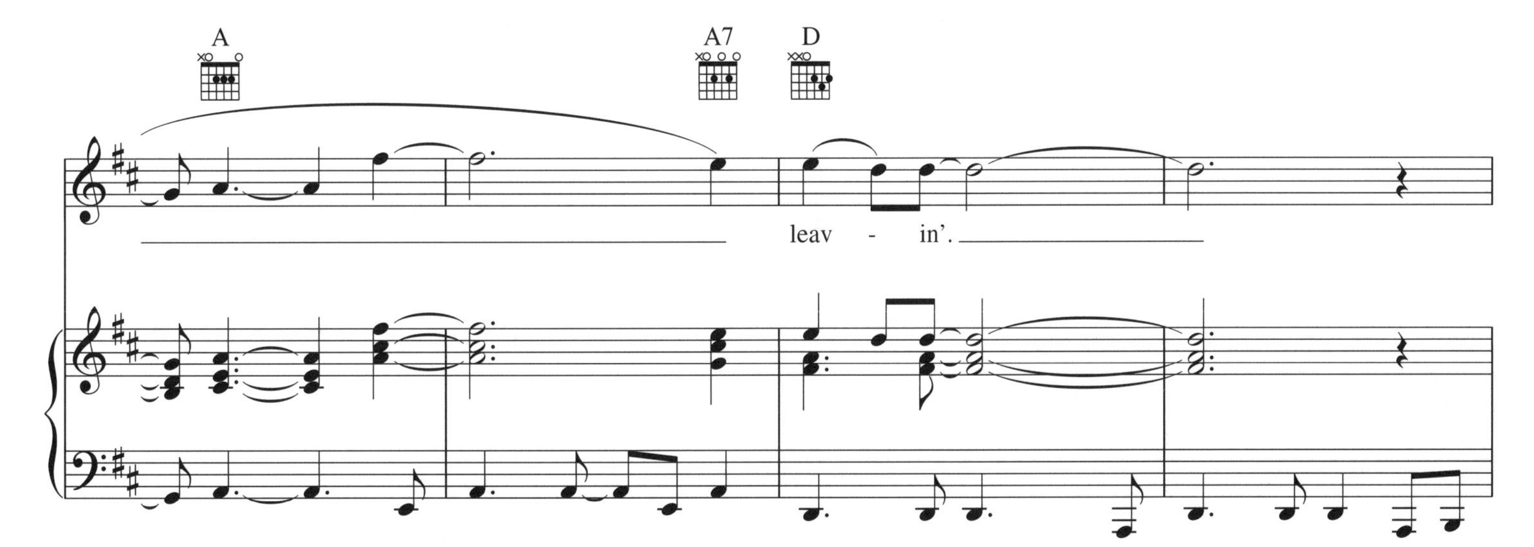
A
A7
D
leav - in'.

D
Am7/D
La, la, la, la, la, la, la, la, la, la, la, la, la.
mp

Gm
3fr
D
2nd time D.S. and Fade
La, la, la, la, la, la, la, la, la, la, la, la, la.

JAILHOUSE ROCK

Words and Music by JERRY LEIBER
and MIKE STOLLER

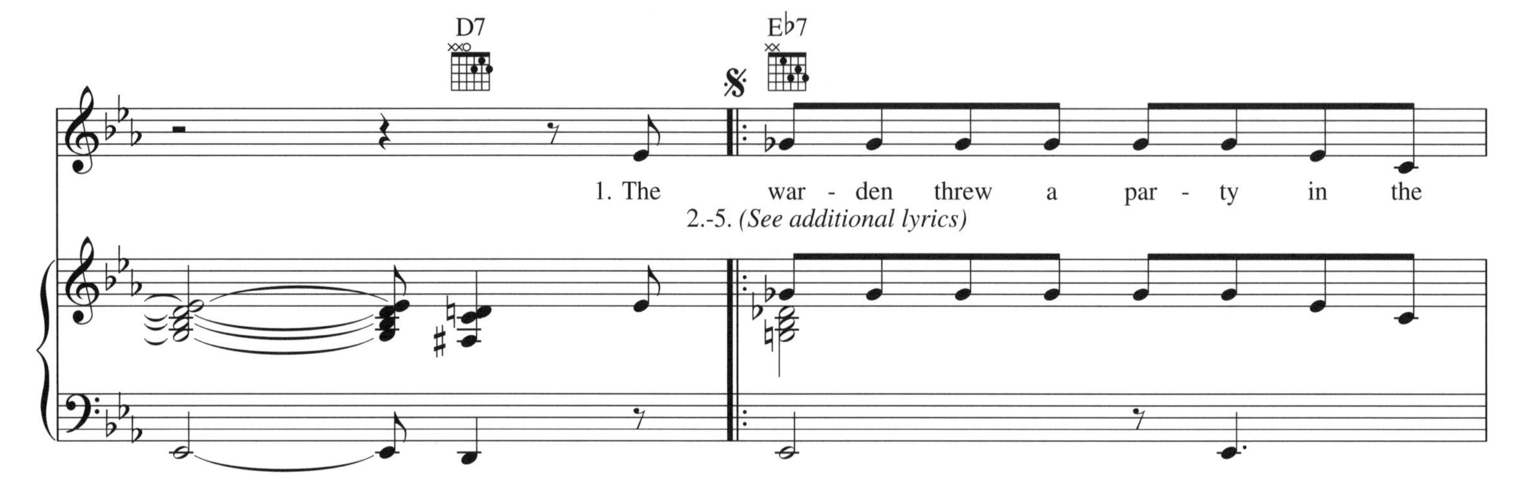

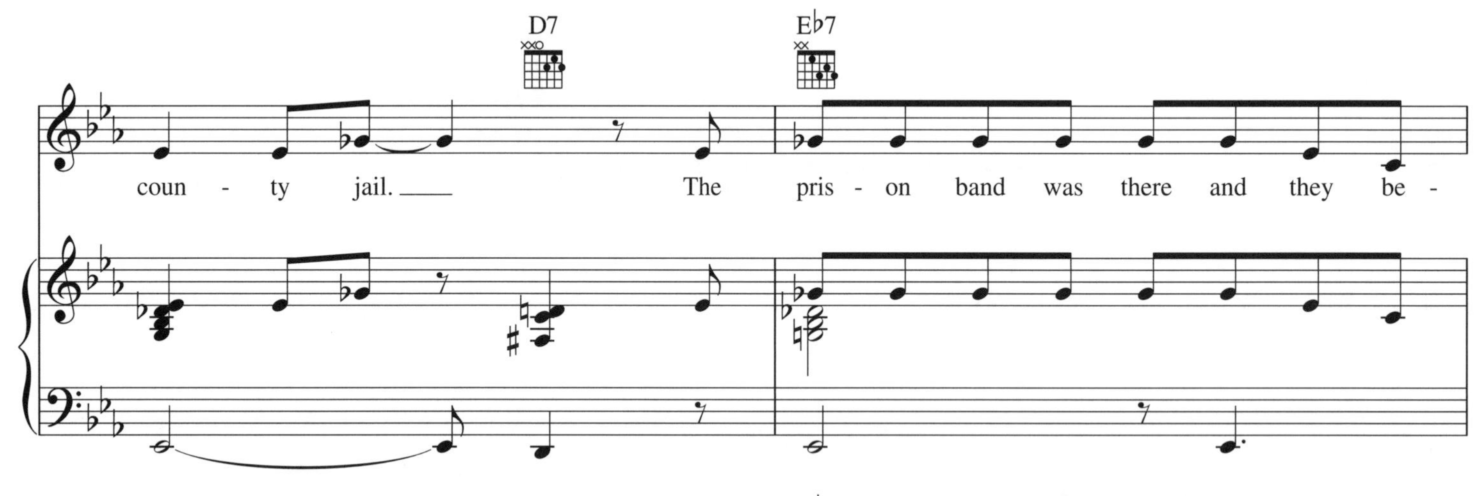

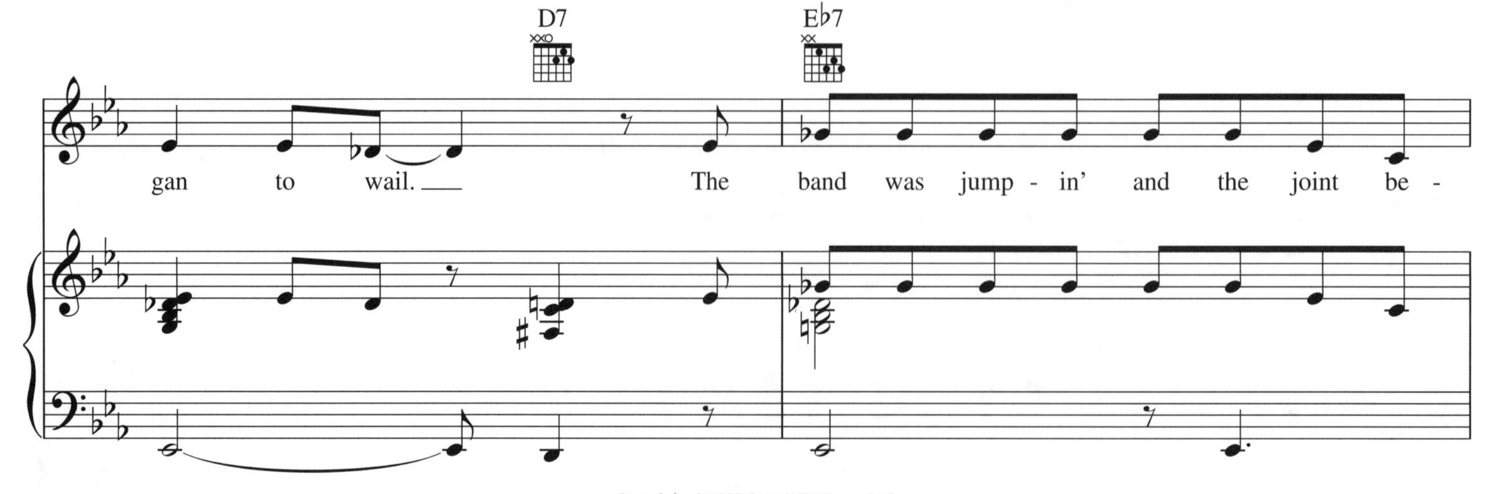

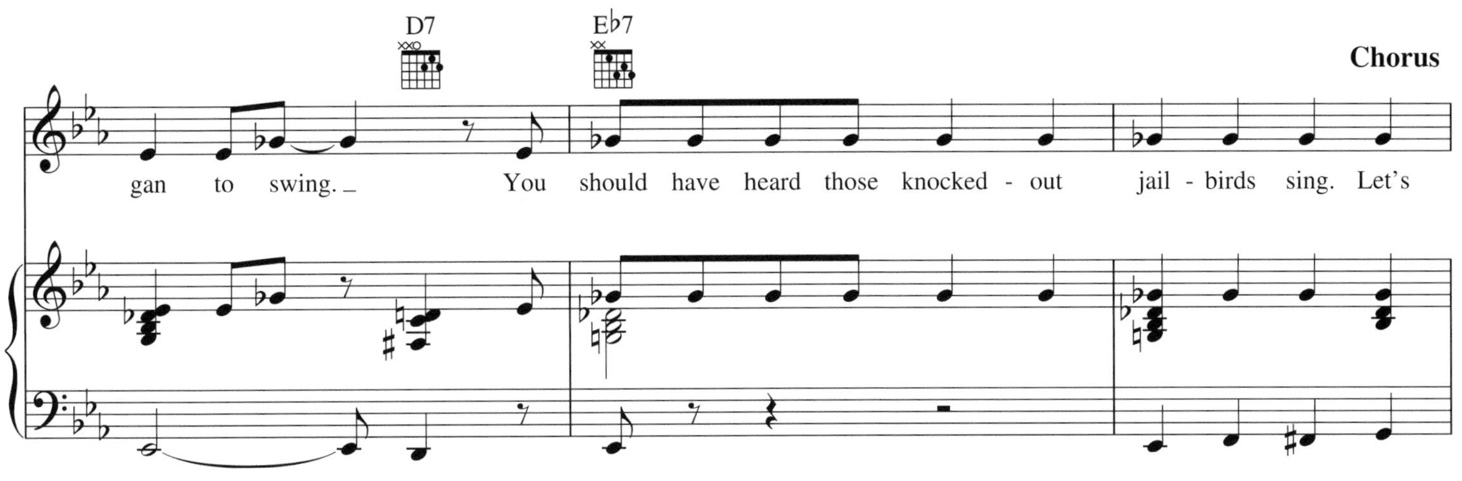

D7
E♭7
Chorus
gan to swing. You should have heard those knocked - out jail - birds sing. Let's

A♭7
4fr
E♭7
rock! Ev - 'ry - bod - y let's rock!

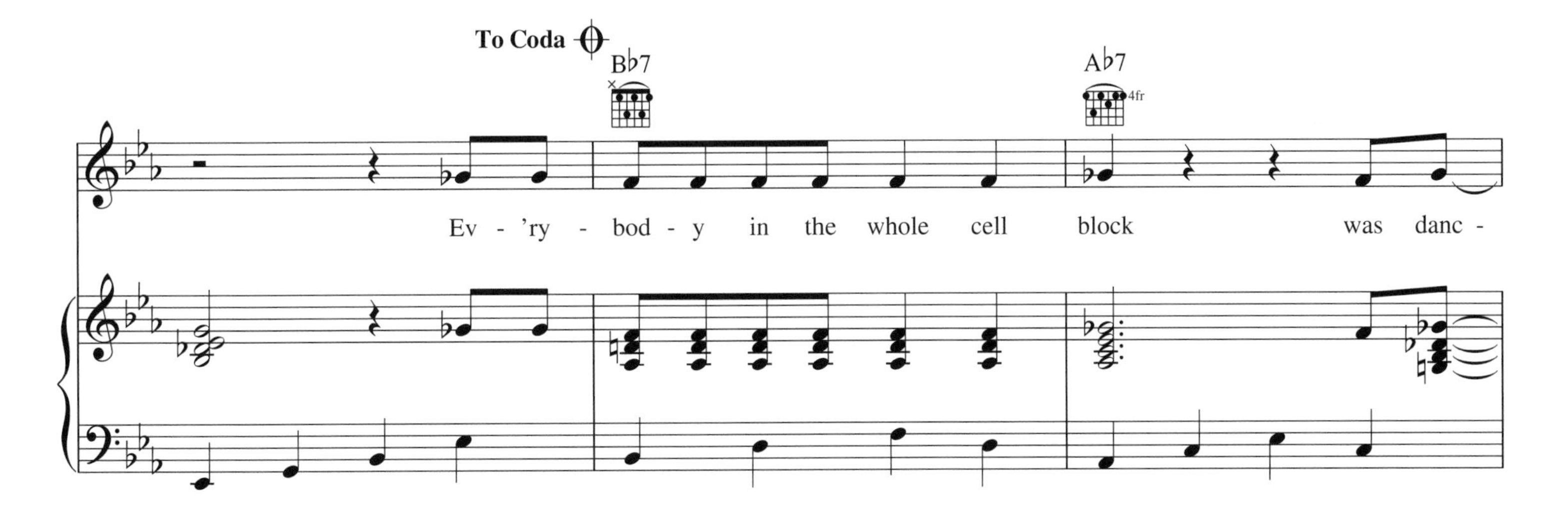

To Coda
B♭7
A♭7
4fr
Ev - 'ry - bod - y in the whole cell block was danc -

1-3
E♭7
D7
4
E♭7
- ing to the Jail - house Rock!
- ing to the Jail - house

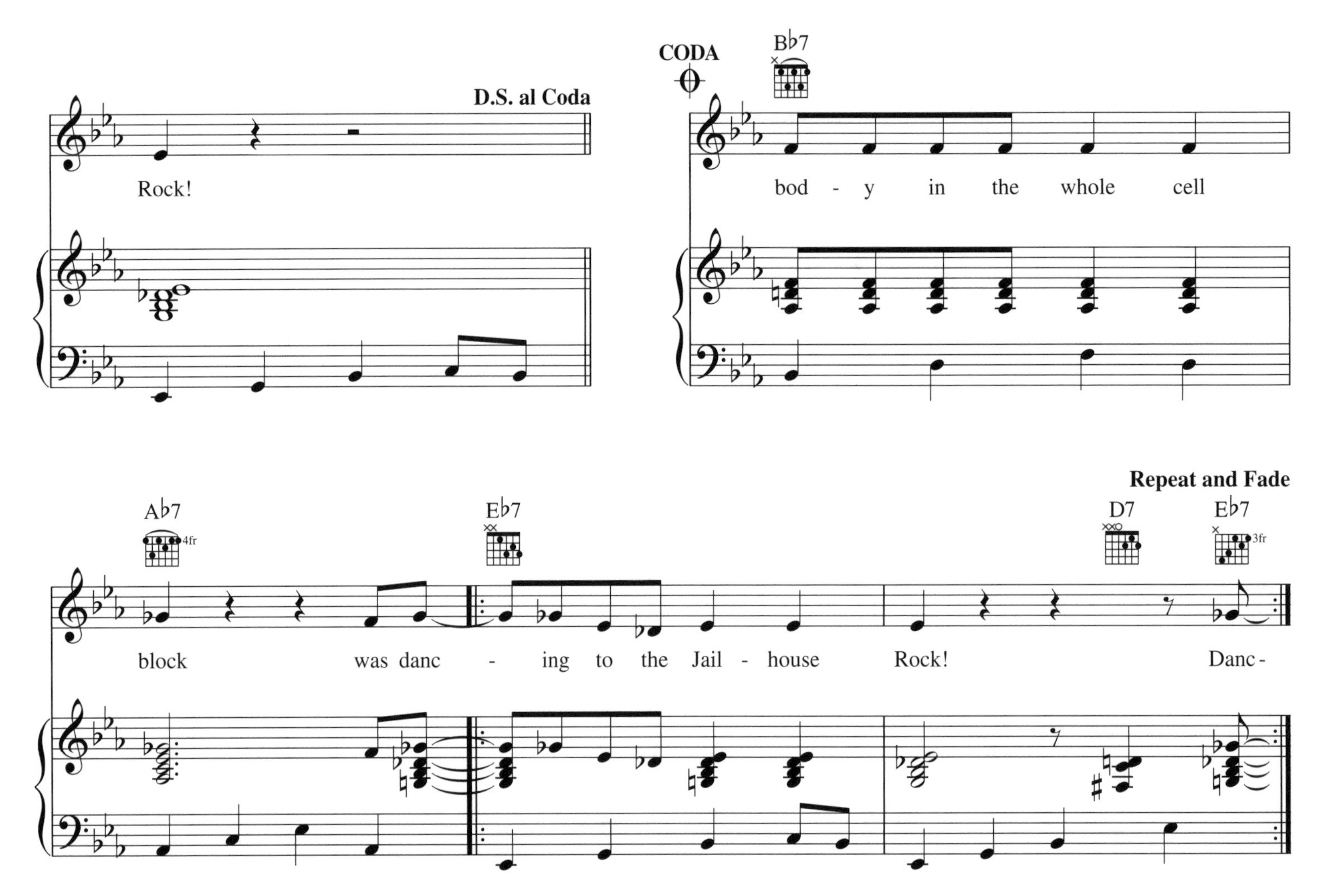

Additional Lyrics

2. Spider Murphy played the tenor saxophone
   Little Joe was blowin' on the slide trombone.
   The drummer boy from Illinois went crash, boom, bang;
   The whole rhythm section was the Purple Gang.
   Chorus

3. Number forty-seven said to number three
   "You're the cutest jailbird I ever did see.
   I sure would be delighted with your company,
   Come on and do the Jailhouse Rock with me."
   Chorus

4. The sad sack was a-sittin' on a block of stone,
   Way over in the corner weeping all alone.
   The warden said: "Hey, Buddy, don't you be no square,
   If you can't find a partner, use a wooden chair!"
   Chorus

5. Shifty Henry said to Bugs: "For heaven's sake,
   No one's lookin', now's our chance to make a break."
   Bugsy turned to Shifty and he said: "Nix, nix;
   I wanna stick around a while and get my kicks."
   Chorus

MEAN WOMAN BLUES

Words and Music by
CLAUDE DeMETRUIS

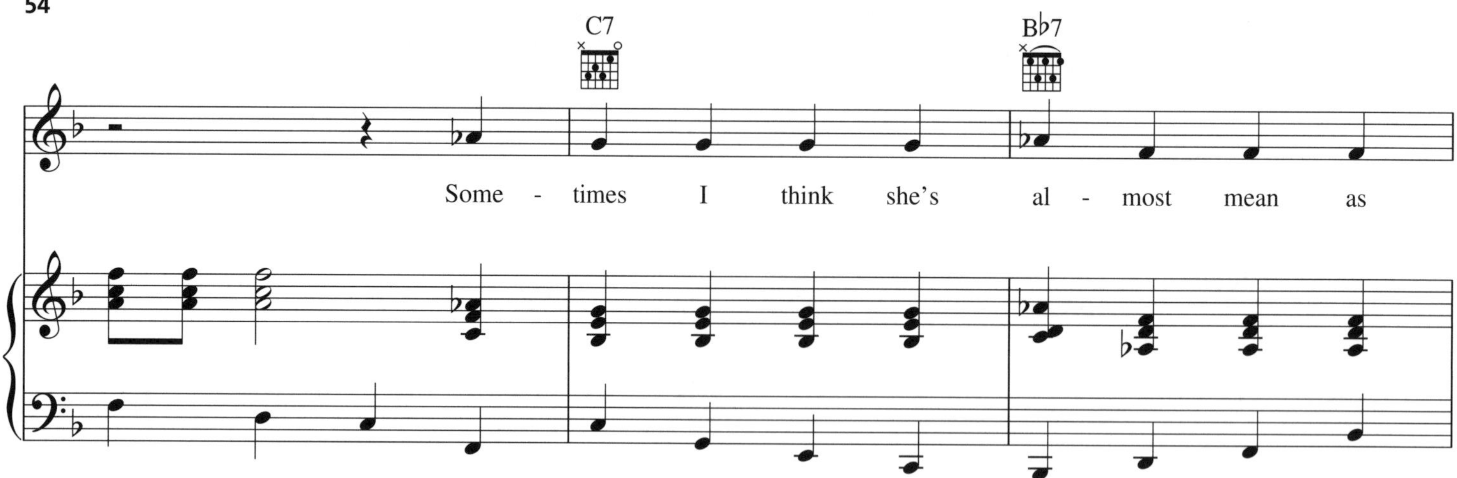
C7
B♭7
Some - times I think she's al - most mean as

F
F
me. A black cat up and
kiss so hard she
strang - est gal I
She makes love with -

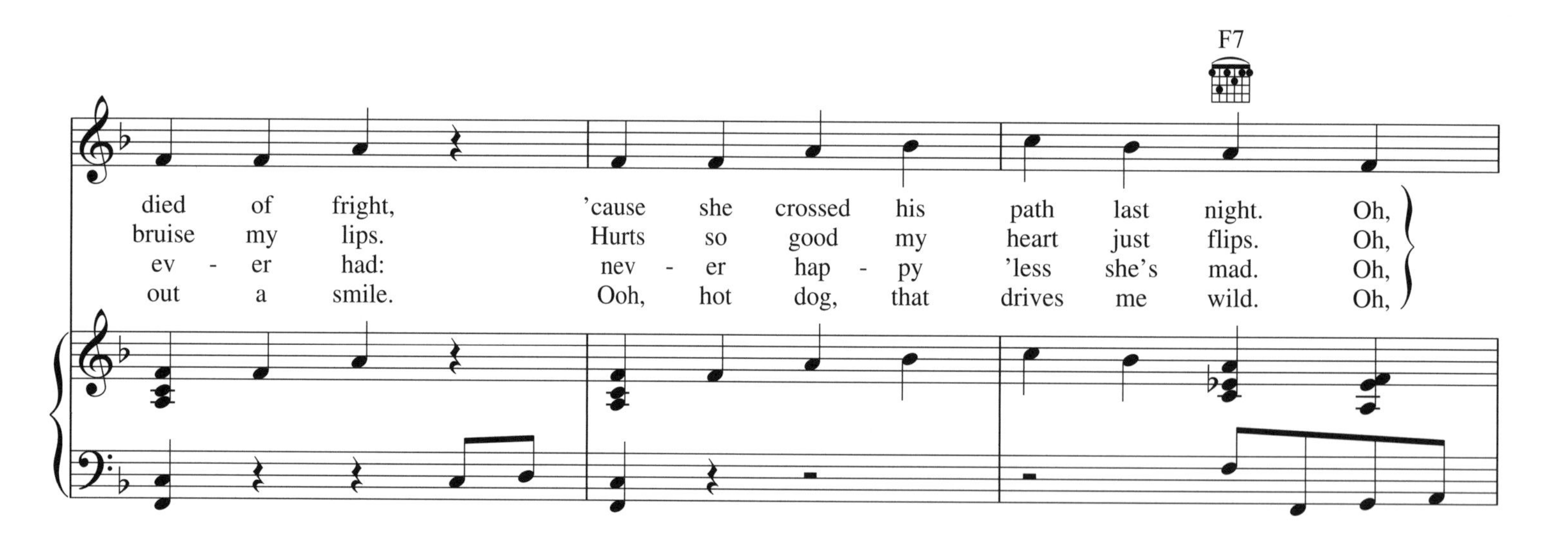
F7
died of fright, 'cause she crossed his path last night. Oh,
bruise my lips. Hurts so good my heart just flips. Oh,
ev - er had: nev - er hap - py 'less she's mad. Oh,
out a smile. Ooh, hot dog, that drives me wild. Oh,

B♭7
F
I got a wom - an mean as she can be.

C7
B♭7
Some - times I think she's al - most mean as

1-3
F
4
F
me.
She
The
me.

C7
B♭7
Some - times I think she's al - most

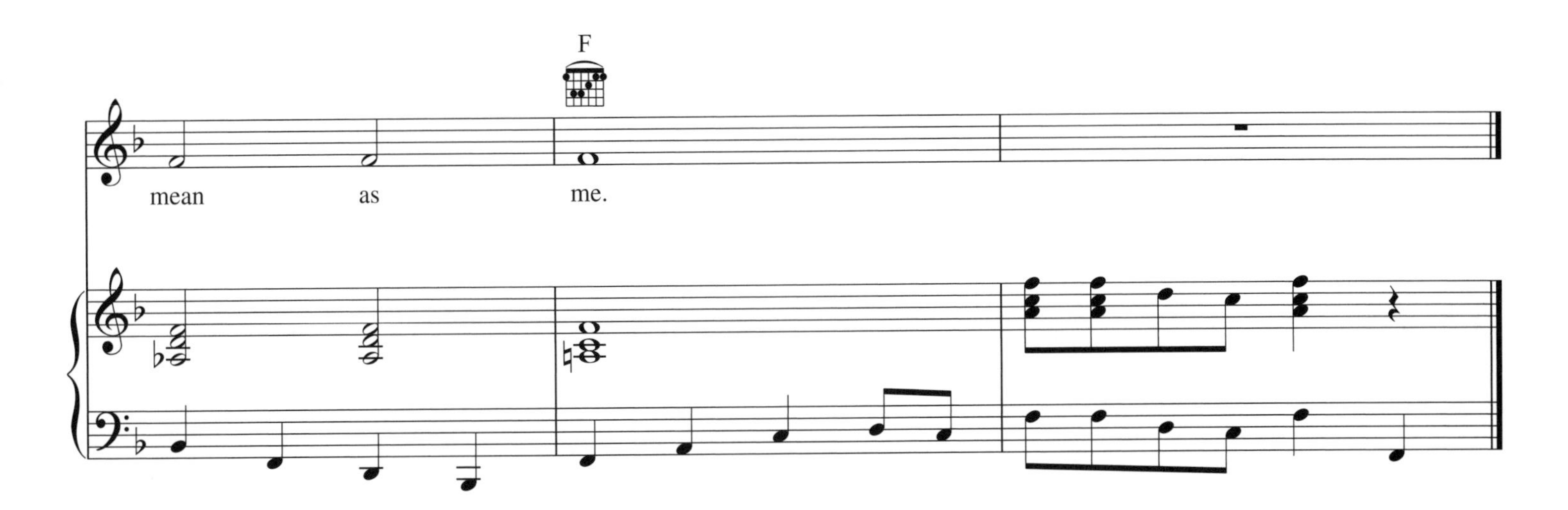
F
mean as me.

LOVE ME TENDER

Words and Music by ELVIS PRESLEY
and VERA MATSON

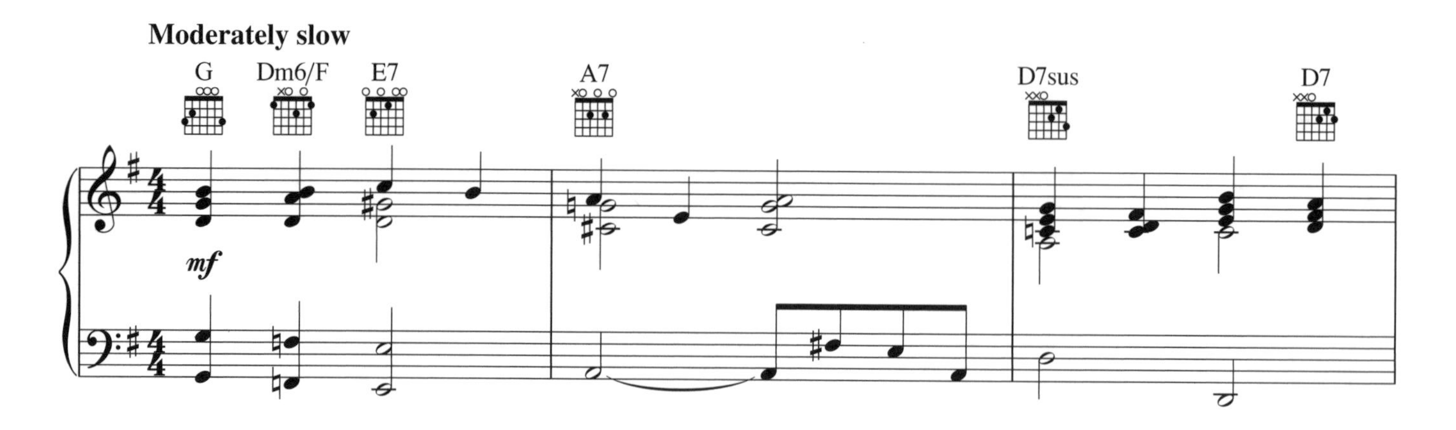

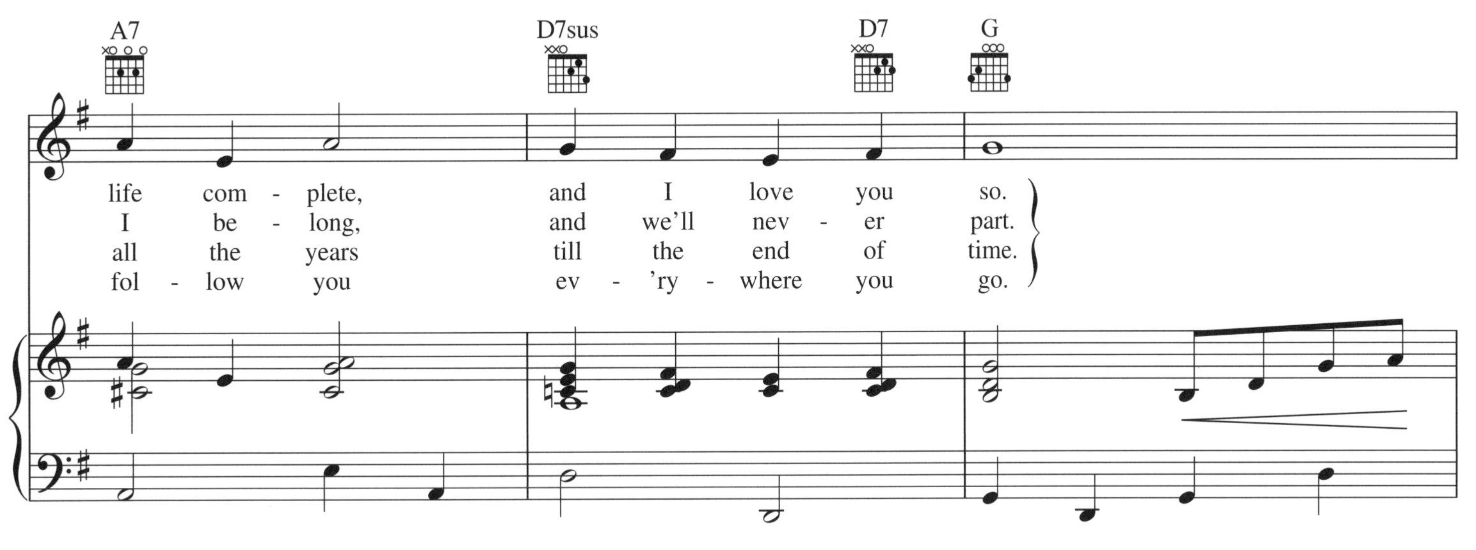
A7
D7sus
D7
G
life com - plete, and I love you so.
I be - long, and we'll nev - er part.
all the years till the end of time.
fol - low you ev - 'ry - where you go.

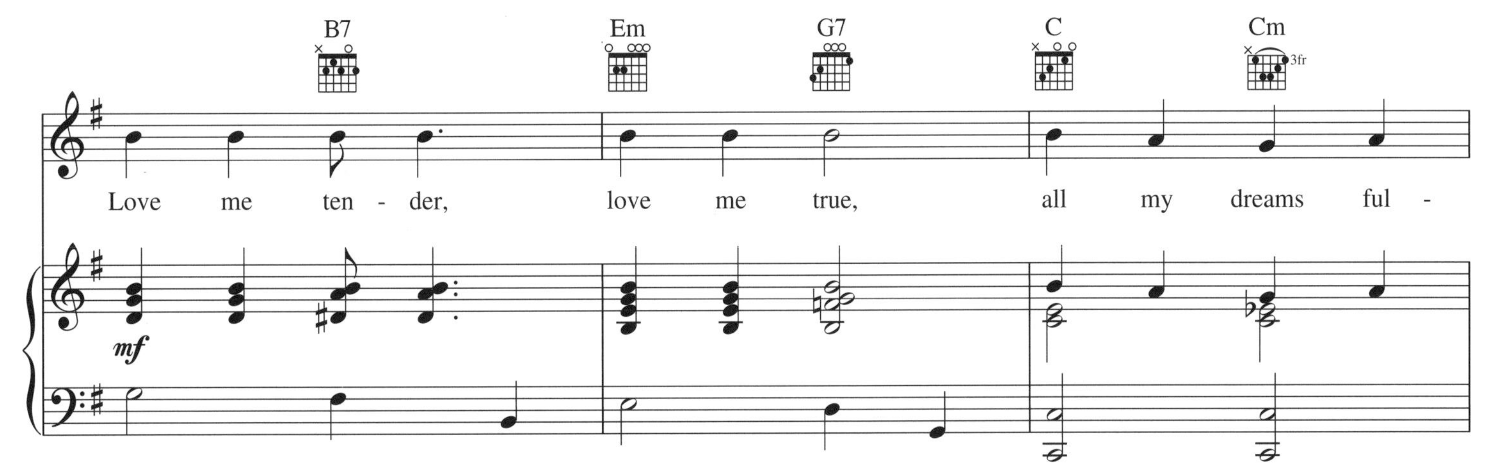
B7
Em
G7
C
Cm
3fr
Love me ten - der, love me true, all my dreams ful -
mf

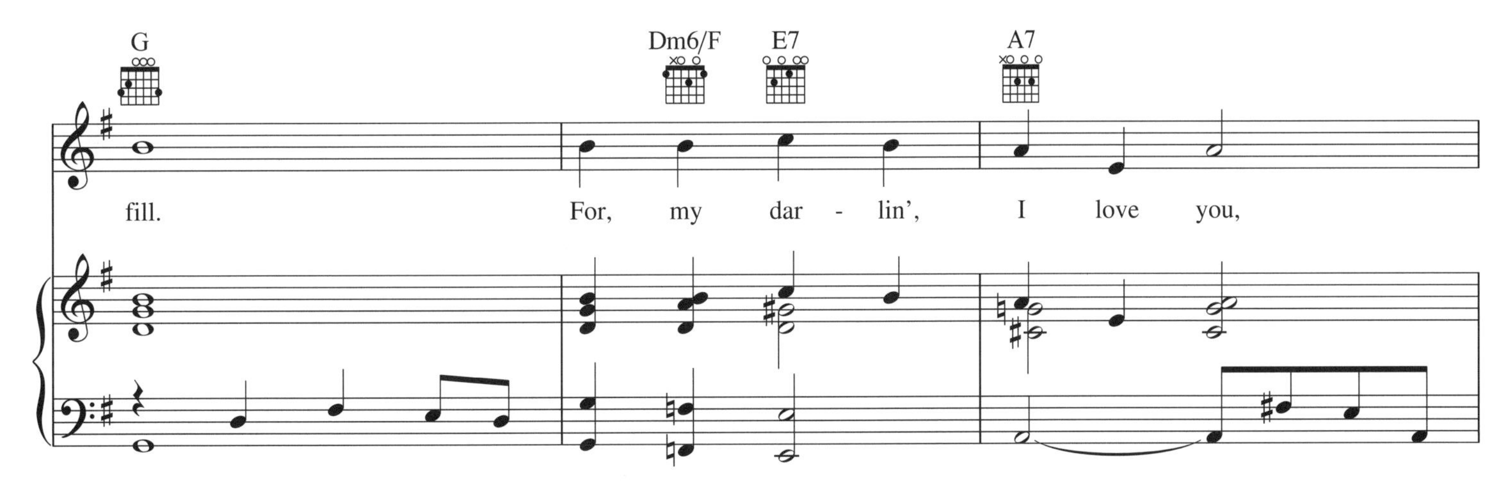
G
Dm6/F
E7
A7
fill. For, my dar - lin', I love you,

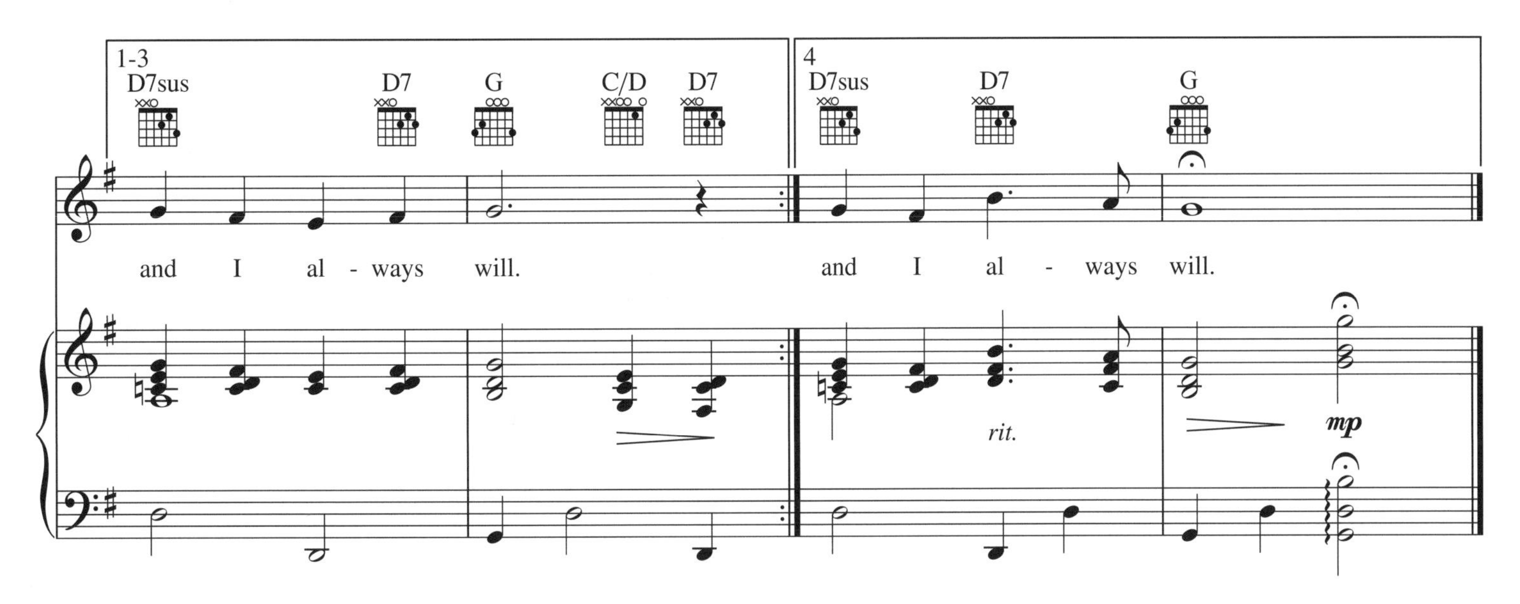
1-3
D7sus
D7
G
C/D
D7
4
D7sus
D7
G
and I al - ways will.
and I al - ways will.
rit.
mp

MOODY BLUE

Words and Music by
MARK JAMES

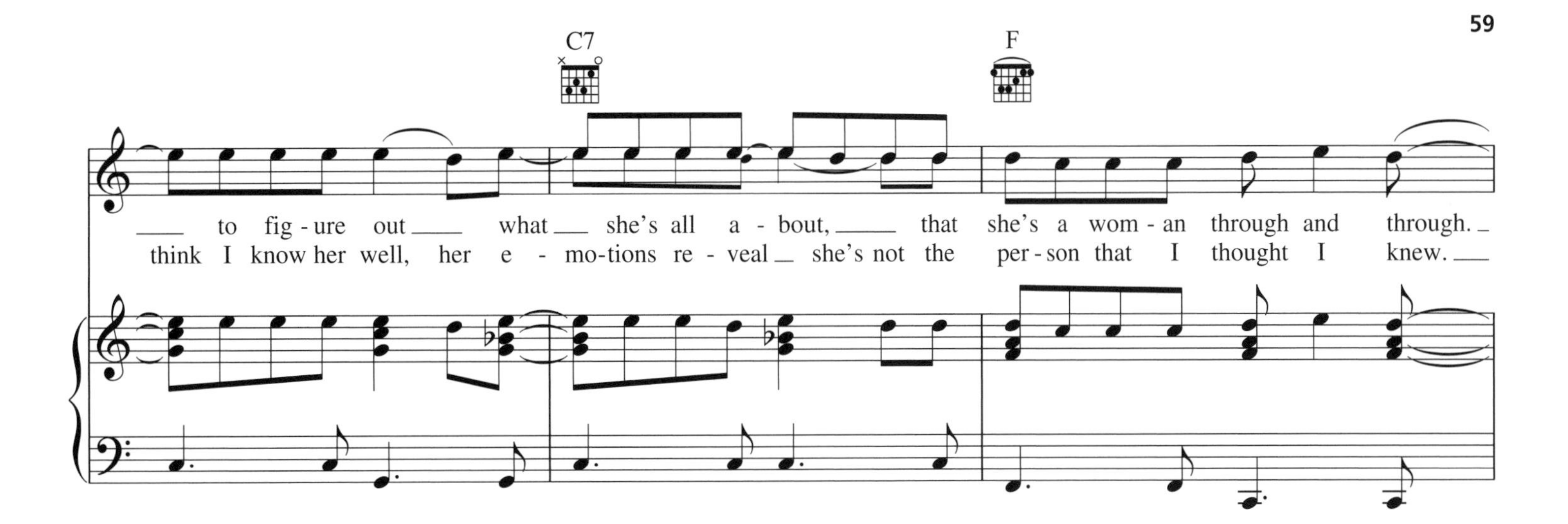

C7
F
to fig-ure out what she's all a-bout, that she's a wom-an through and through.
think I know her well, her e-mo-tions re-veal she's not the per-son that I thought I knew.

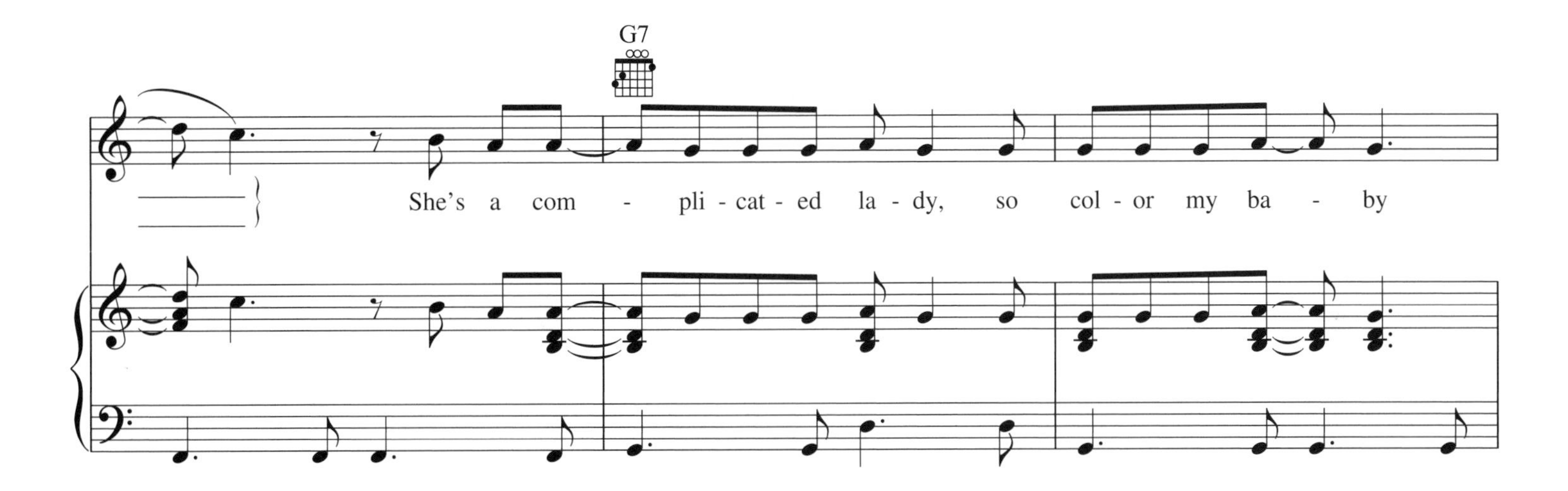

G7
She's a com-pli-cat-ed la-dy, so col-or my ba-by

C
G7
C
mood-y blue. Oh, mood-y blue, tell me am I

Dm7
G7
get-tin' through. I keep hang-in' on try-na

C
G7
learn the song but I nev - er do.
Oh,

C
Dm7
mood - y blue,
tell me who I'm talk - in' to.

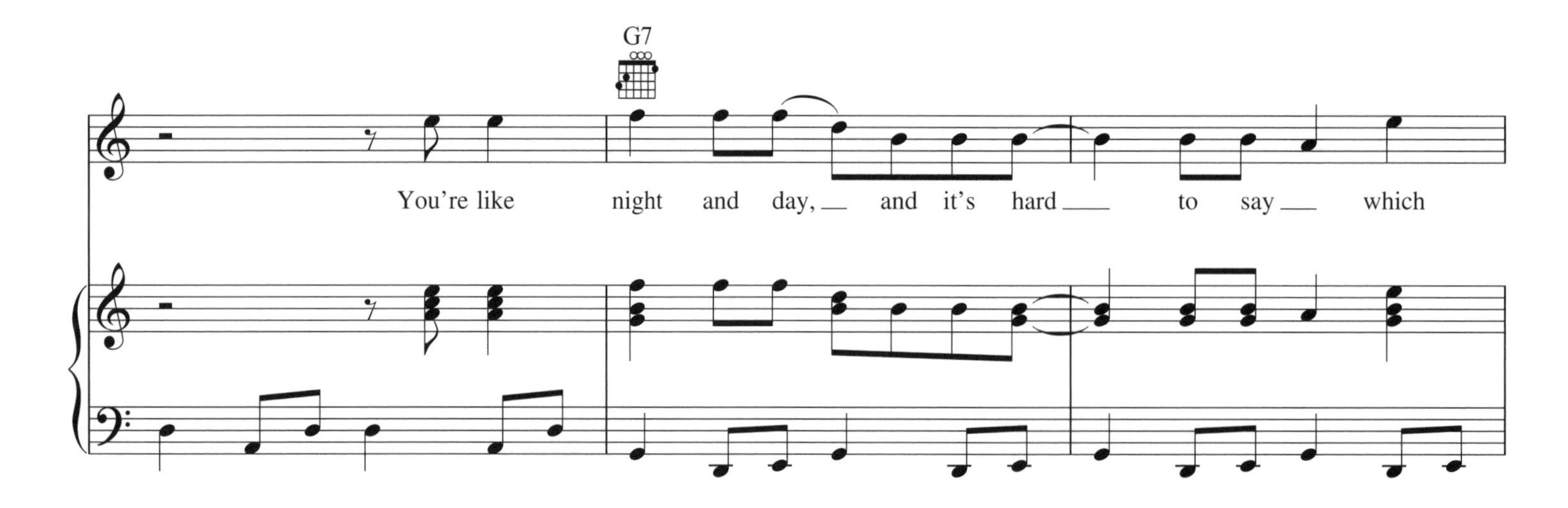
G7
You're like night and day, and it's hard to say which

C
1
Dm7
G7
2
G7
D.S. and Fade
one is you.
Well, when Mon -
Oh,

(Let Me Be Your)
TEDDY BEAR

Words and Music by KAL MANN
and BERNIE LOWE

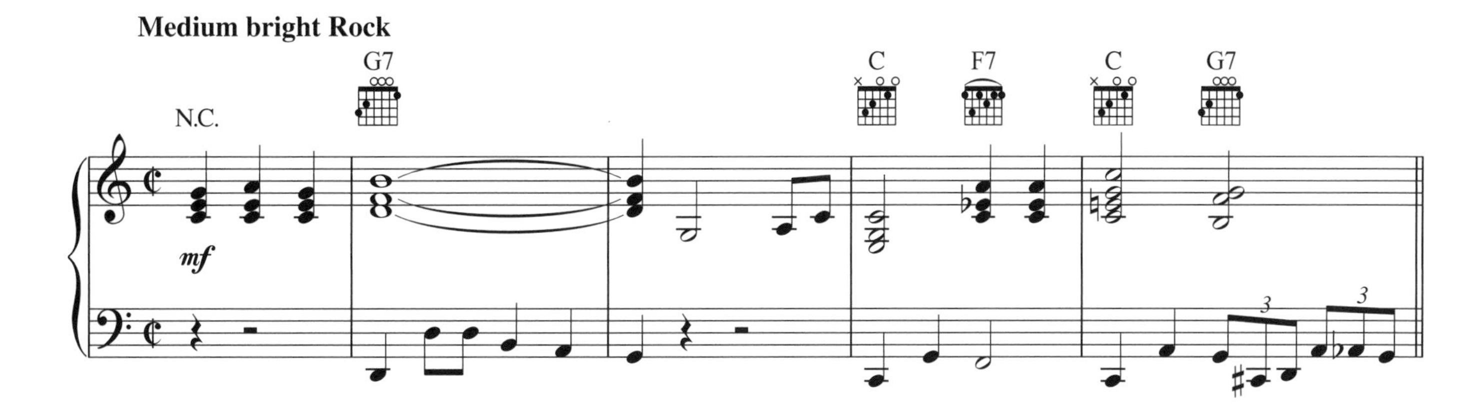

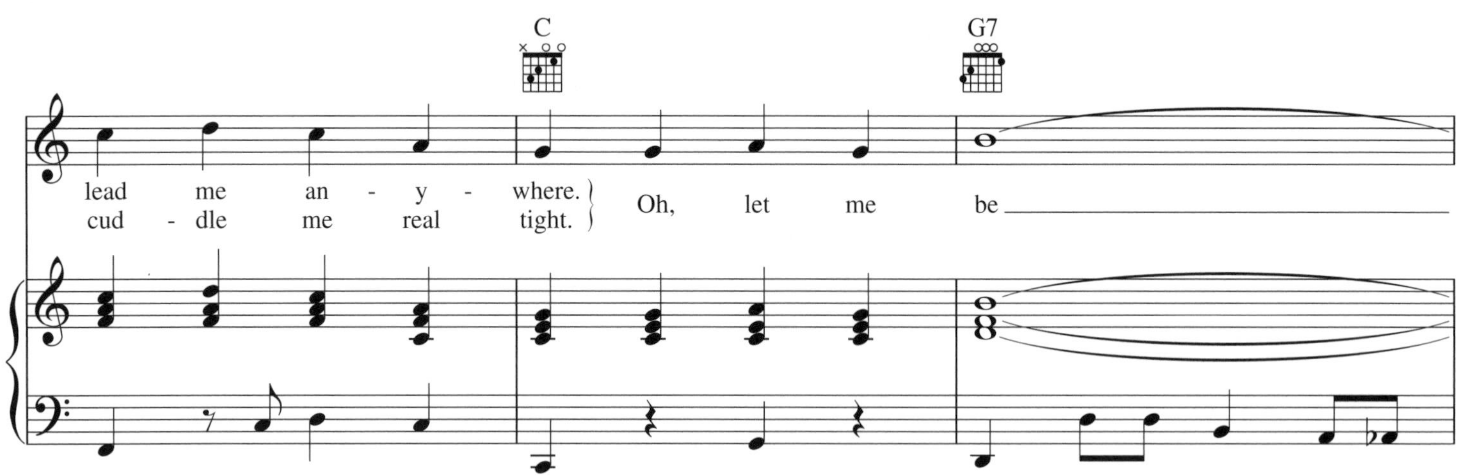
C
G7
lead me an - y - where.
cud - dle me real tight.
Oh, let me be

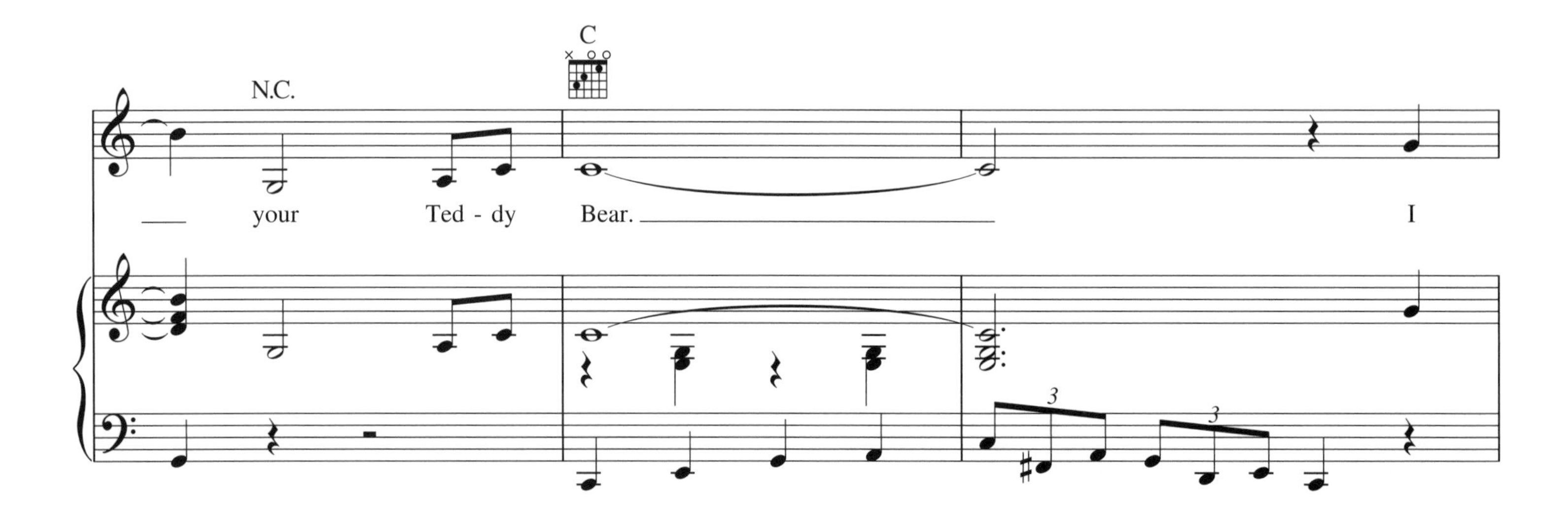
N.C.
C
your Ted - dy Bear.
I

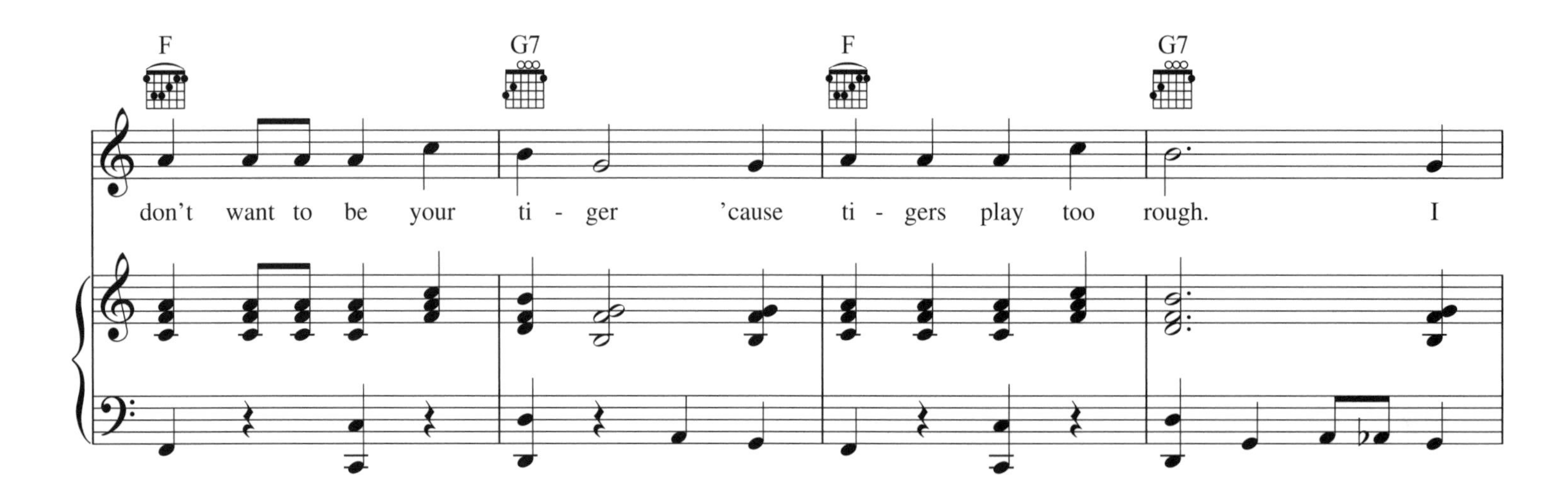
F
G7
F
G7
don't want to be your ti - ger 'cause ti - gers play too rough.
I

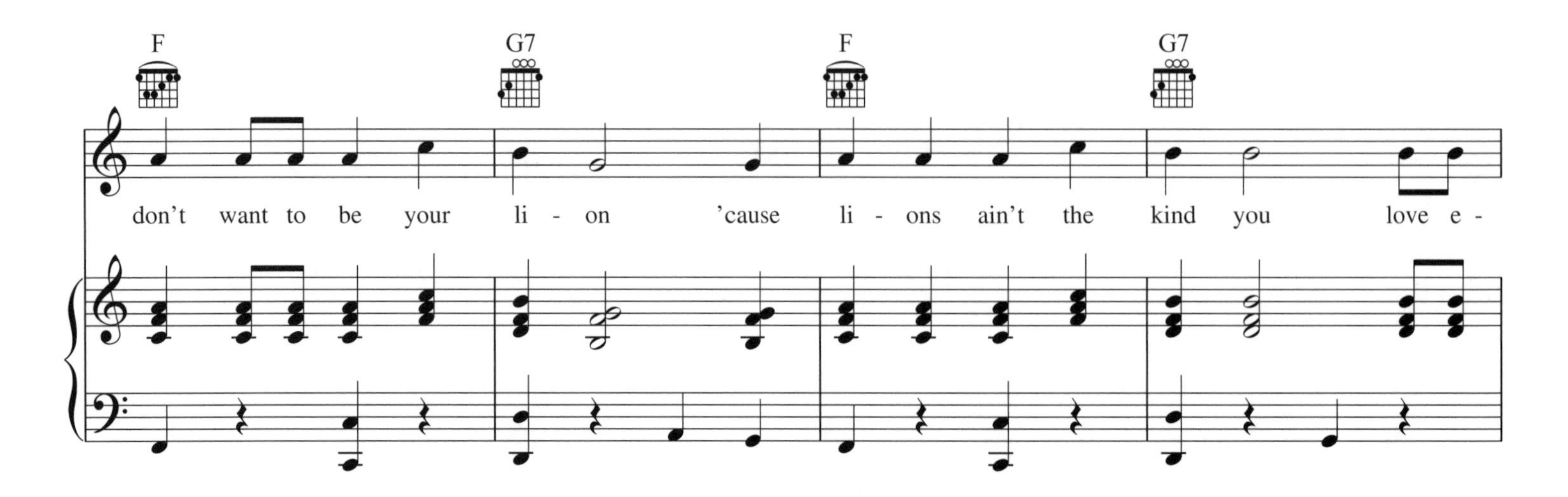
F
G7
F
G7
don't want to be your li - on 'cause li - ons ain't the kind you love e -

C
N.C.
C
nough. Just wan - na be your Ted - dy

F
Bear. Put a chain a - round my neck and

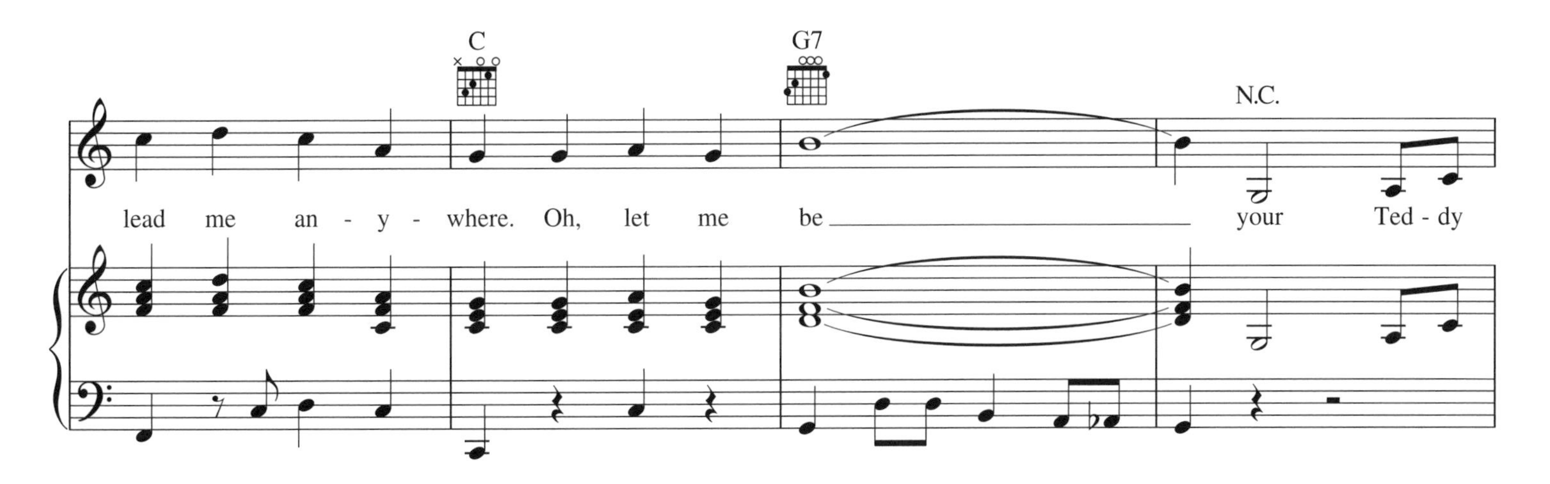
C
G7
N.C.
lead me an - y - where. Oh, let me be your Ted - dy

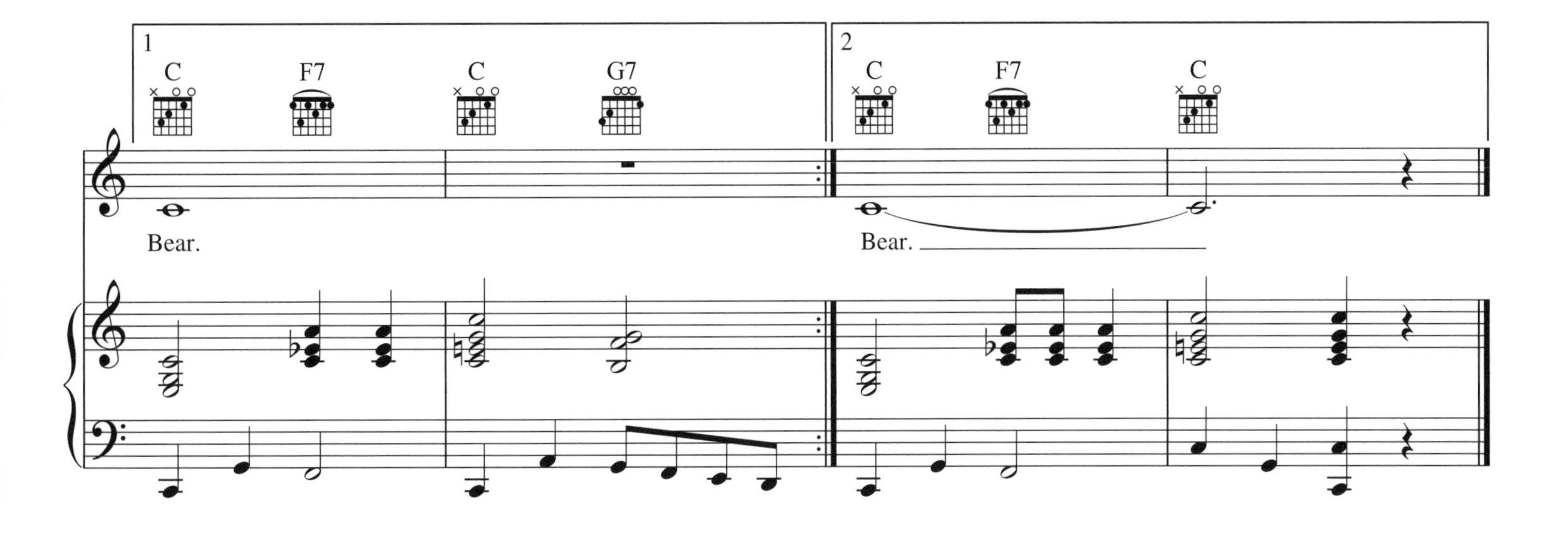
1
C F7 C G7
Bear.
2
C F7 C
Bear.

MY BABY LEFT ME

Words and Music by
ARTHUR CRUDUP

Moderately bright

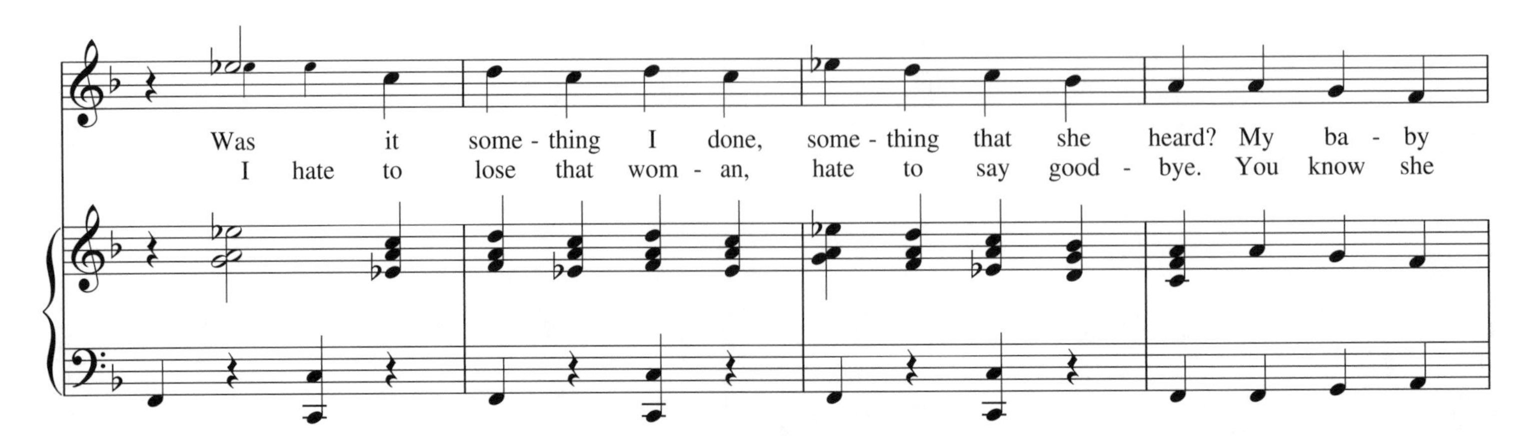

Additional Lyrics

3. Baby, one of these mornings, Lord, it won't be long,
You'll look for me and, baby, and daddy he'll be gone.
You know you left me, you know you left me.
My baby even left me, never said goodbye.

4. Now, I stand at my window, wring my hands and moan.
All I know is that the one I love is gone.
My baby left me, you know she left me.
My baby even left me, never said a word.

PLEDGING MY LOVE

Words and Music by DON ROBEY
and FATS WASHINGTON

Gm
C7
F
B♭
B♭6
soul, dear, for - ev - er burn. My heart's at your com - mand, dear, to

B♭m7
B♭m6
F/C
A7/C♯
Dm
keep, love and to hold. Mak - ing you hap - py's my de - sire, dear, keep - ing

G7
C7
F
C7
you is my goal. I'll for - ev - er love you, the rest of my days. I'll nev - er part

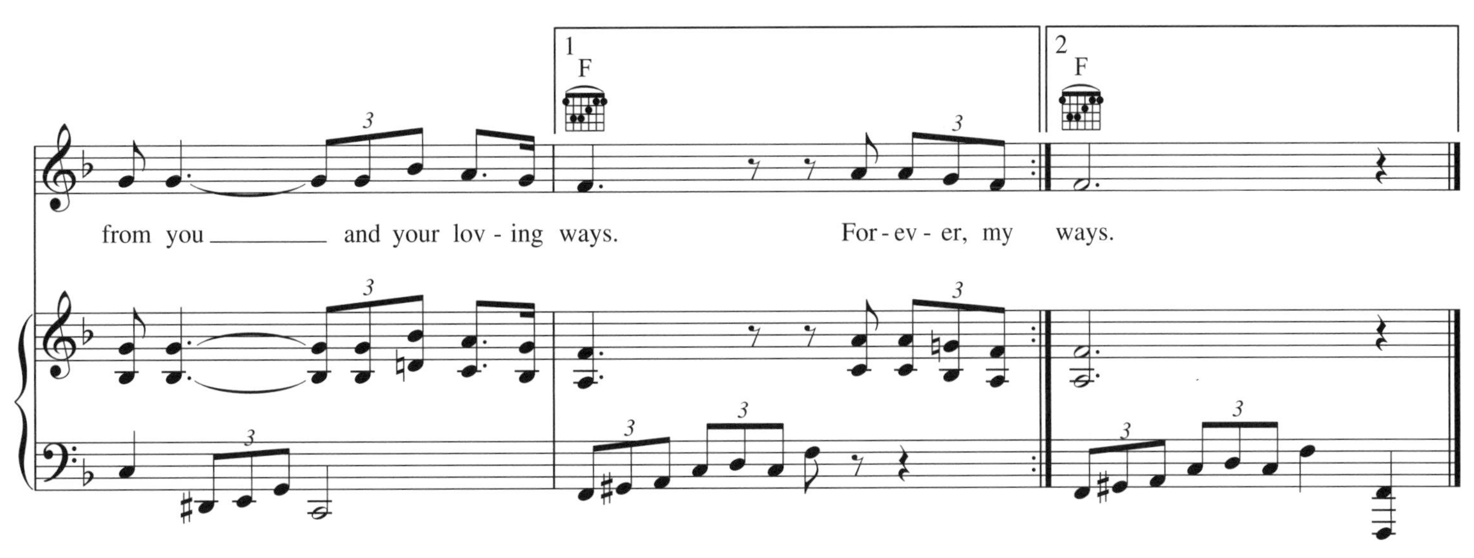
F
F
from you and your lov - ing ways. For - ev - er, my ways.

TREAT ME NICE

Words and Music by JERRY LEIBER
and MIKE STOLLER

F♯dim7
G7
C
Don't - cha ev - er kiss me once; kiss me twice.
If you don't want me to be cold as ice,

D7
G7
C
Treat me nice
treat me nice.

1
2
F
I
Make me feel at home

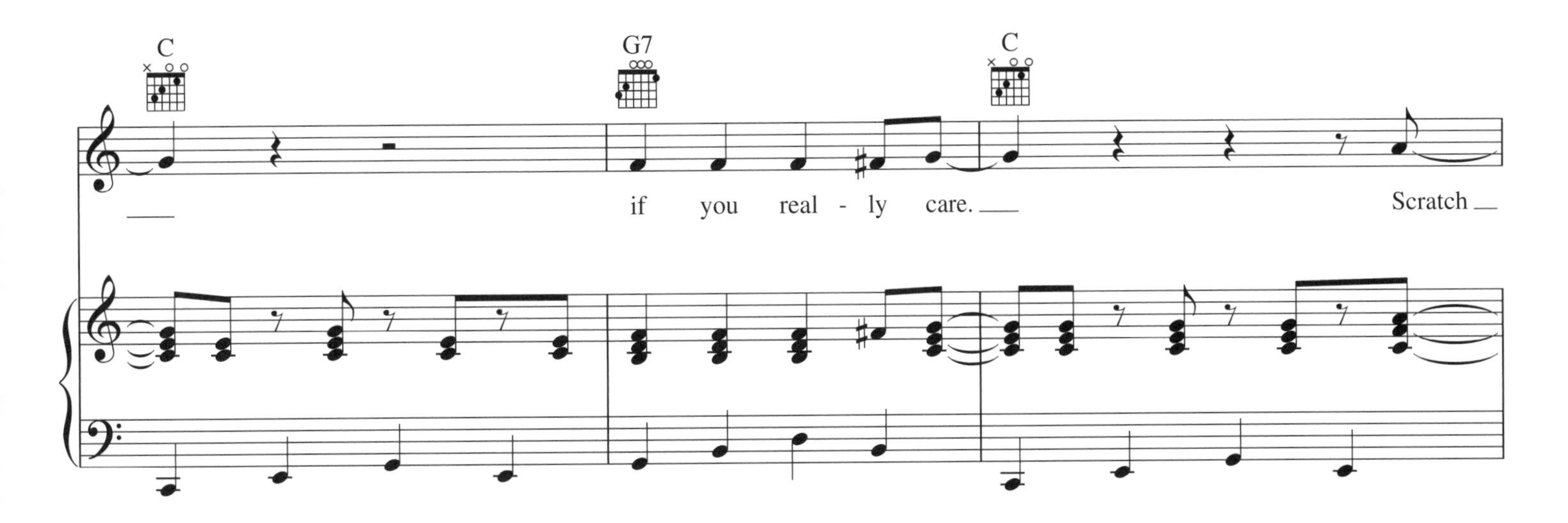

C
G7
C
if you real - ly care.
Scratch

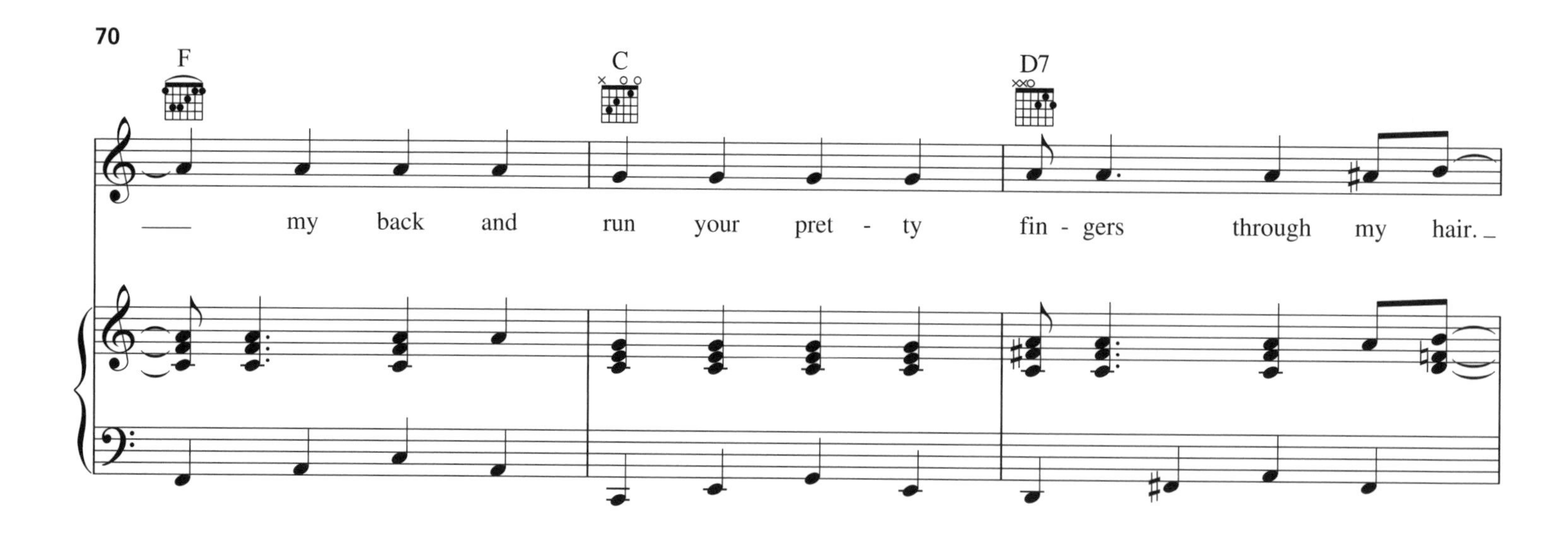
F
C
D7
my back and run your pret - ty fin - gers through my hair.

G7
C
You know I'll be your slave

F
if you ask me to.
But if you don't be - have,

F♯dim7
I'll walk right out on you.
If you

G7
C
D7
want my love, then take my ad - vice:

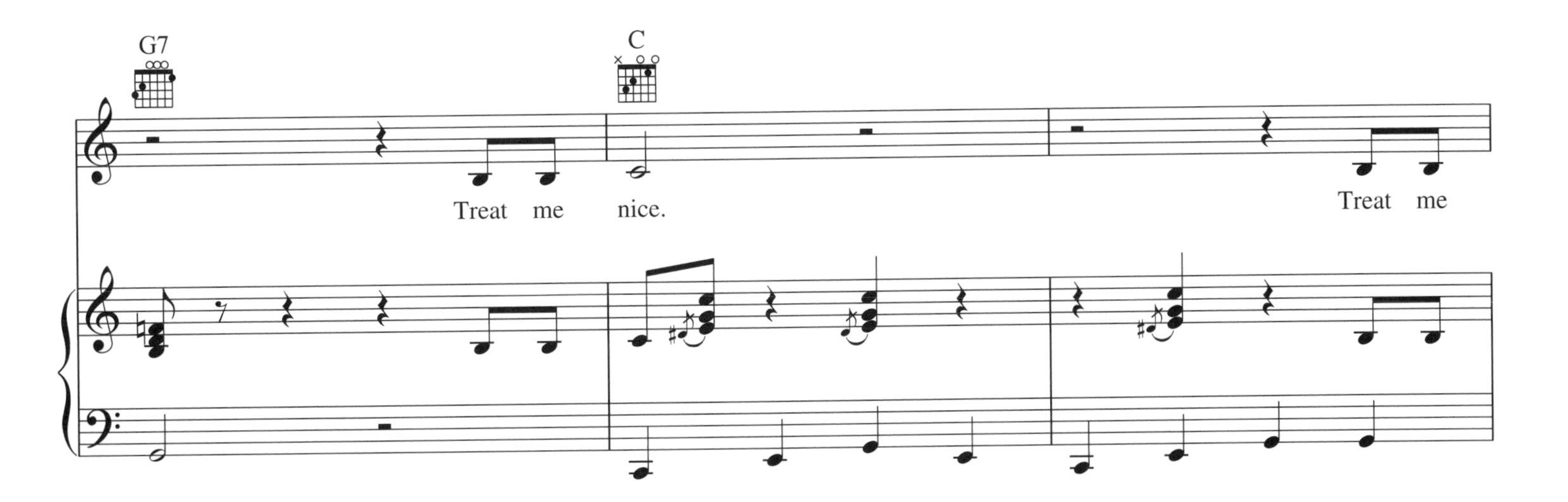
G7
C
Treat me nice.
Treat me

D7
nice.
If you real - ly want my

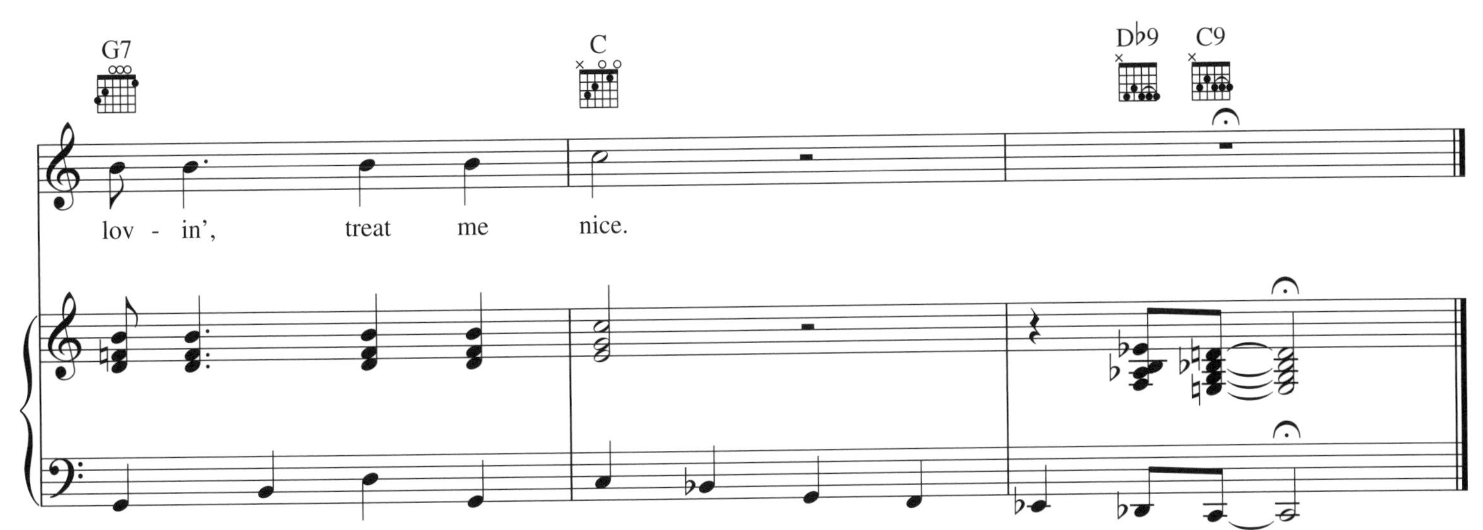
G7
C
D♭9
C9
lov - in', treat me nice.

WEAR MY RING AROUND YOUR NECK

Words and Music by BERT CARROLL
and RUSSELL MOODY

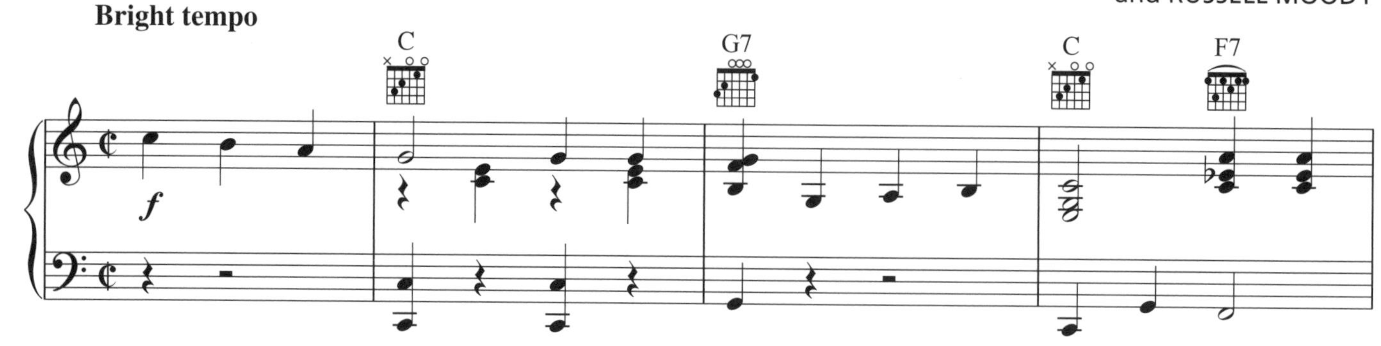

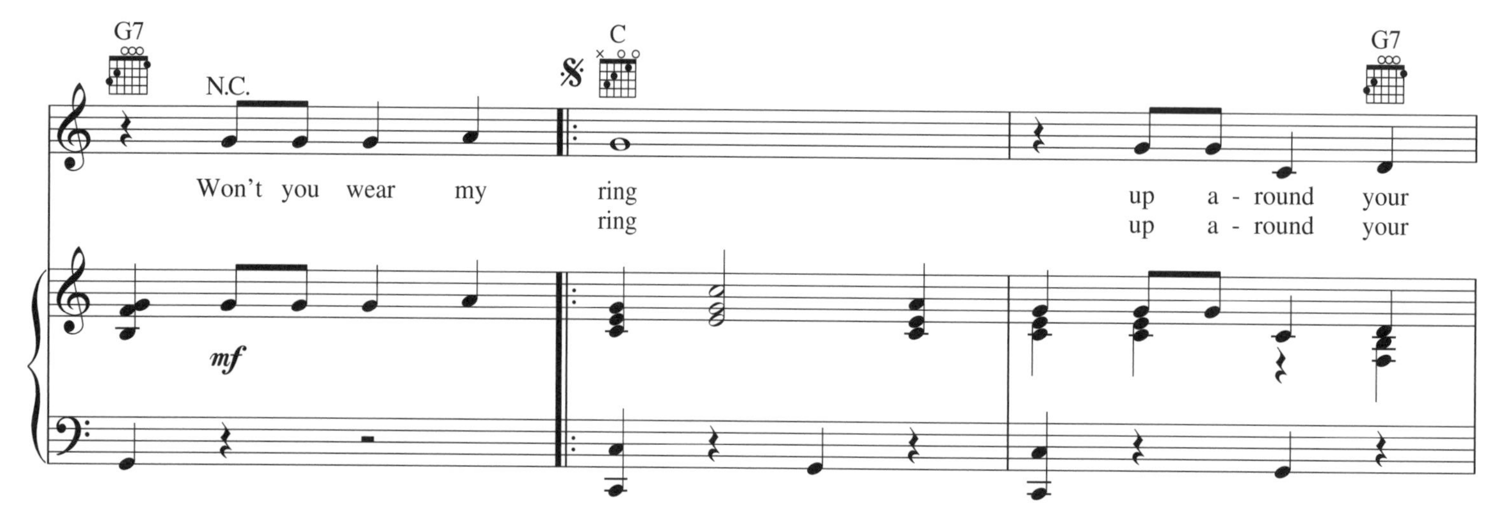

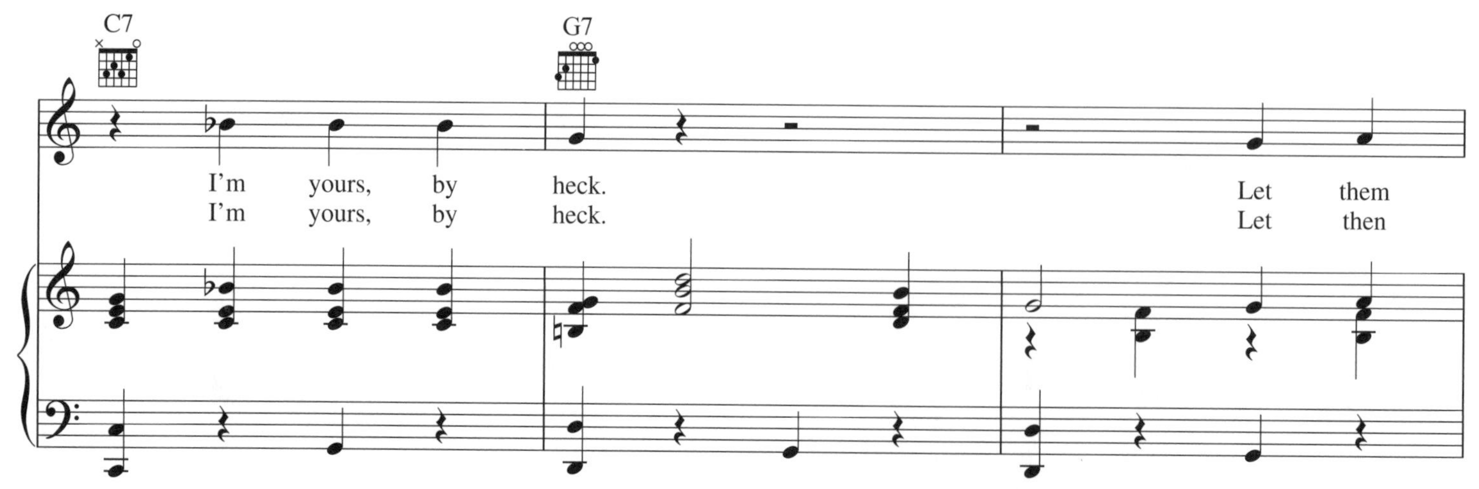

C
C7
F
see your love for me,
know I love you so,

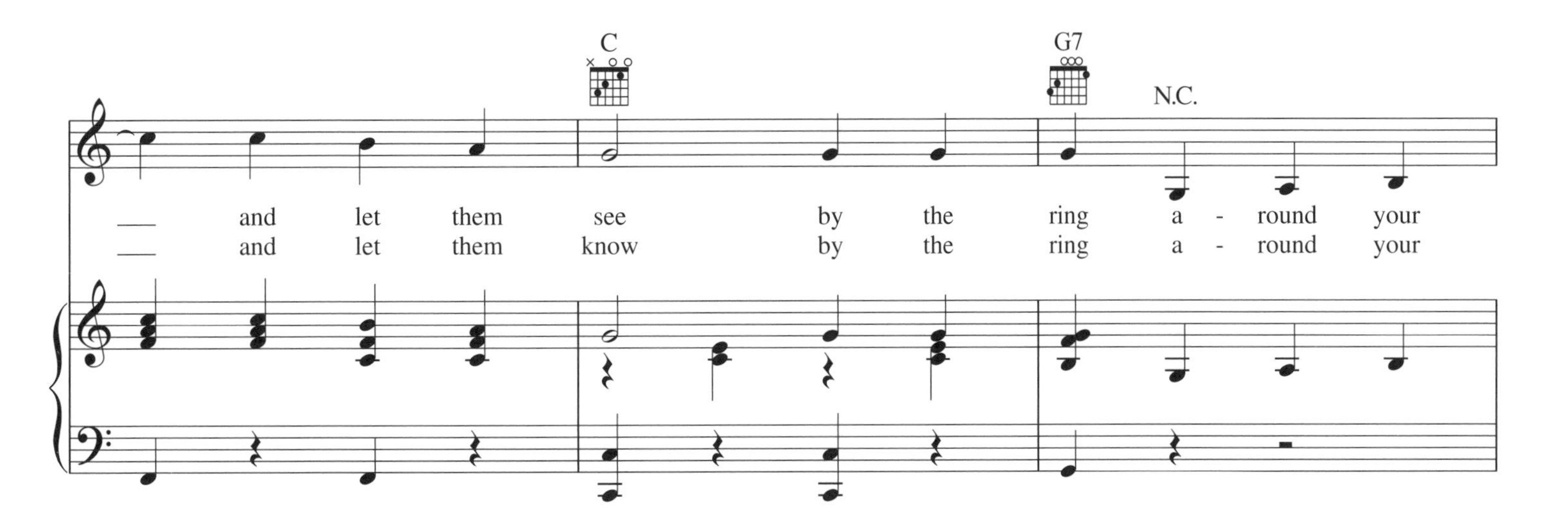
C
G7
N.C.
and let them see by the ring a - round your
and let them know by the ring a - round your

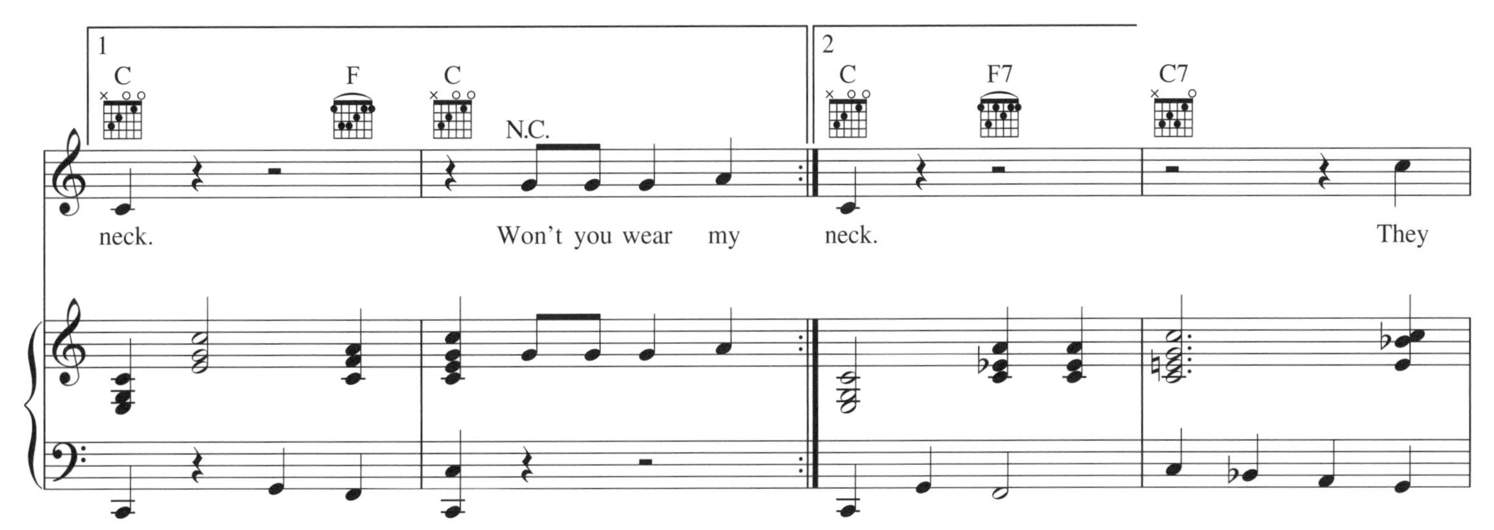
1
2
C
F
C
N.C.
C
F7
C7
neck. Won't you wear my neck. They

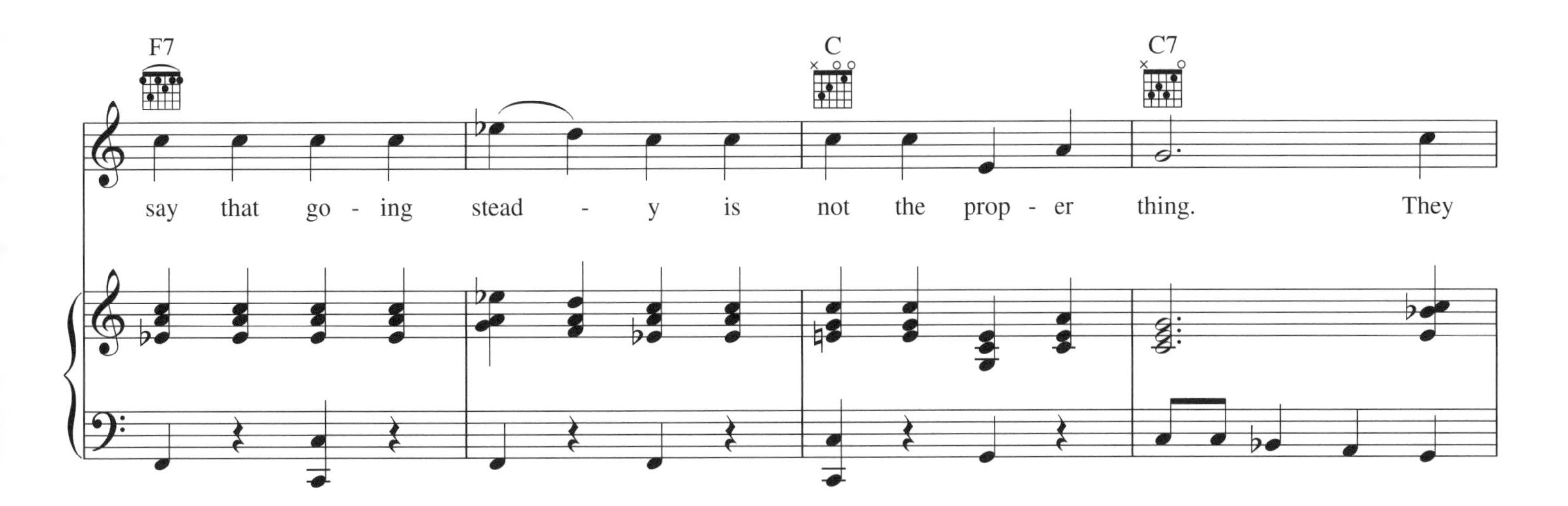
F7
C
C7
say that go - ing stead - y is not the prop - er thing. They

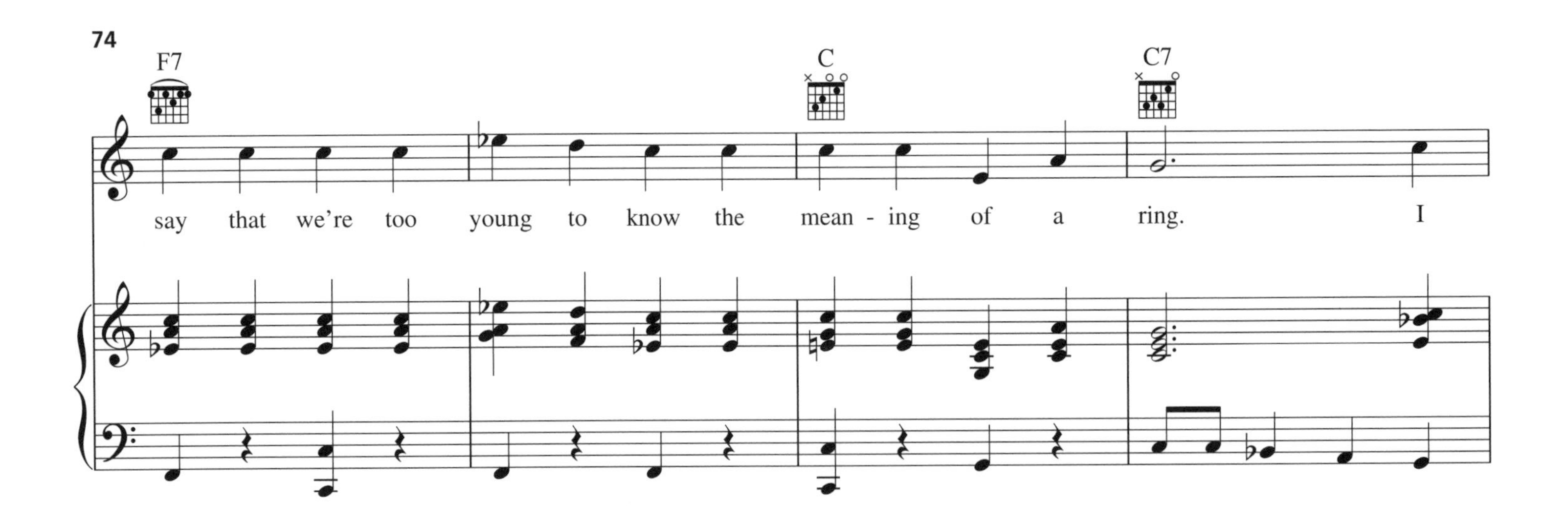
F7
C
C7
say that we're too young to know the mean - ing of a ring. I

F7
C
on - ly know I love you and that you love me, too. So,

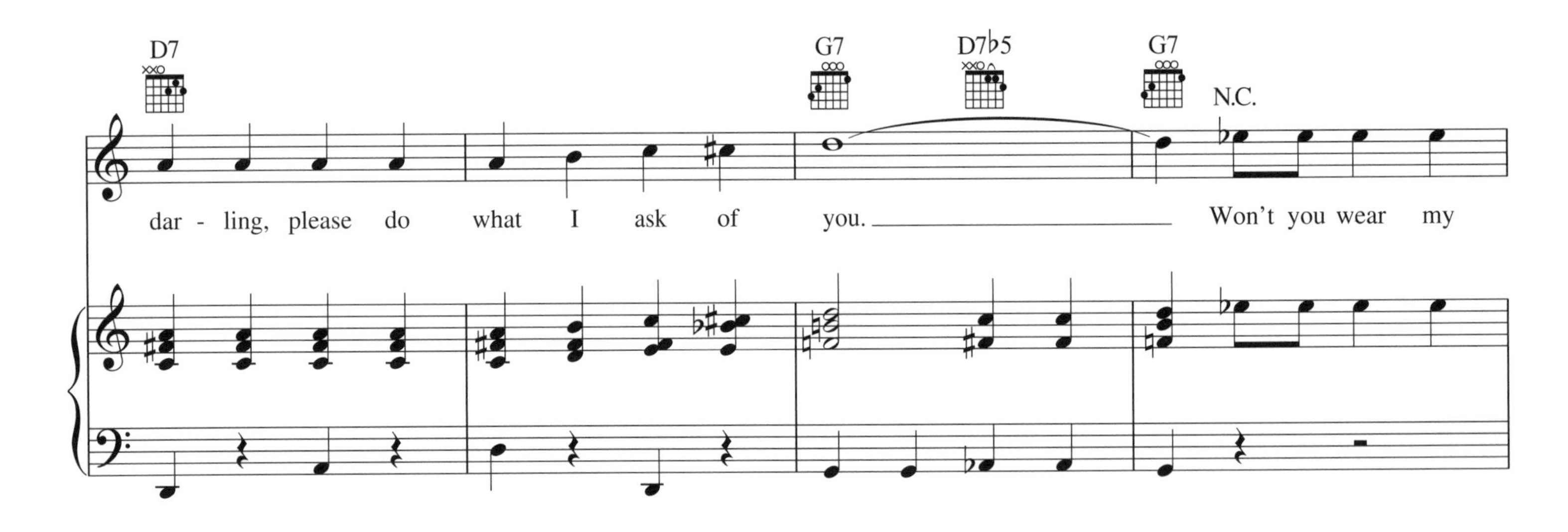
D7
G7
D7♭5
G7
N.C.
dar - ling, please do what I ask of you. Won't you wear my

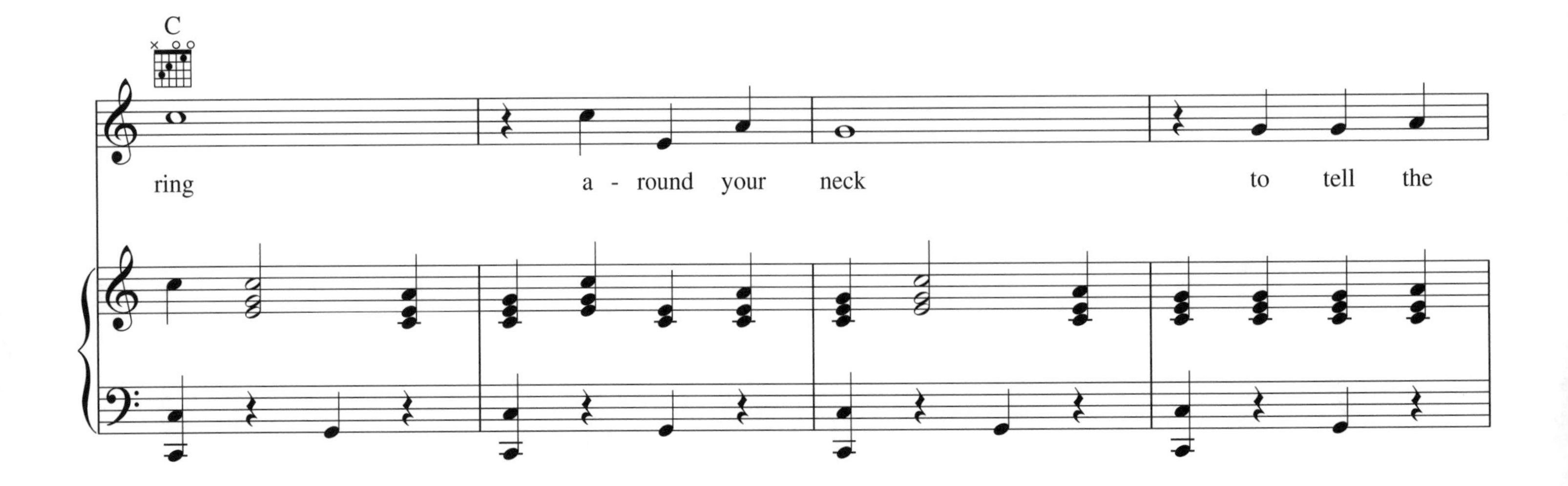
C
ring a - round your neck to tell the

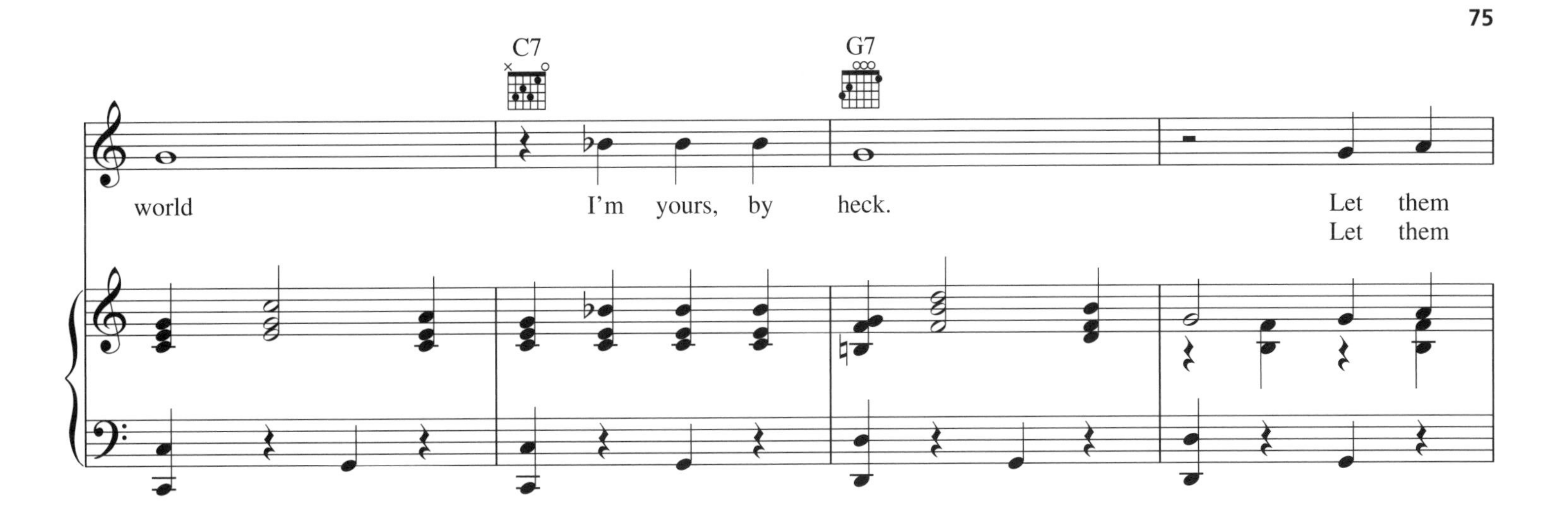
C7
G7
world
I'm yours, by
heck.
Let them
Let them

C
C7
F
see
know
your love for
I love you
me,
so,

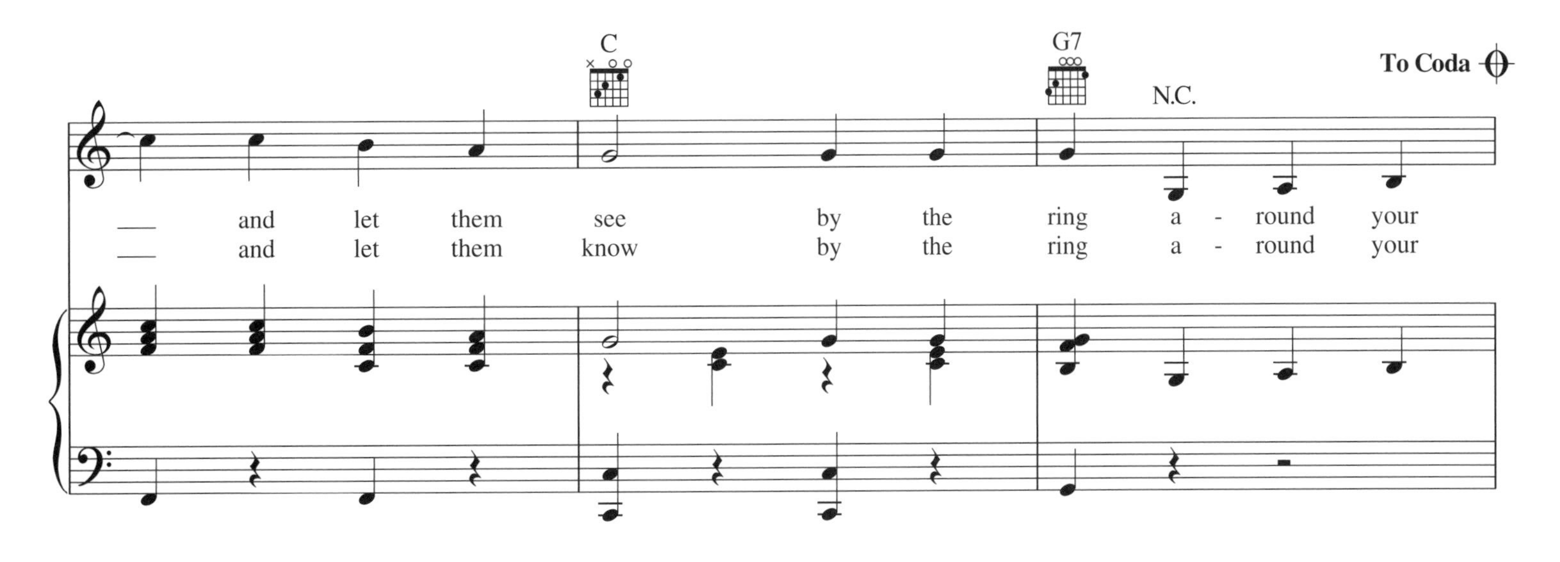
C
G7
To Coda
N.C.
and let them see
and let them know
by the
ring a - round your
ring a - round your

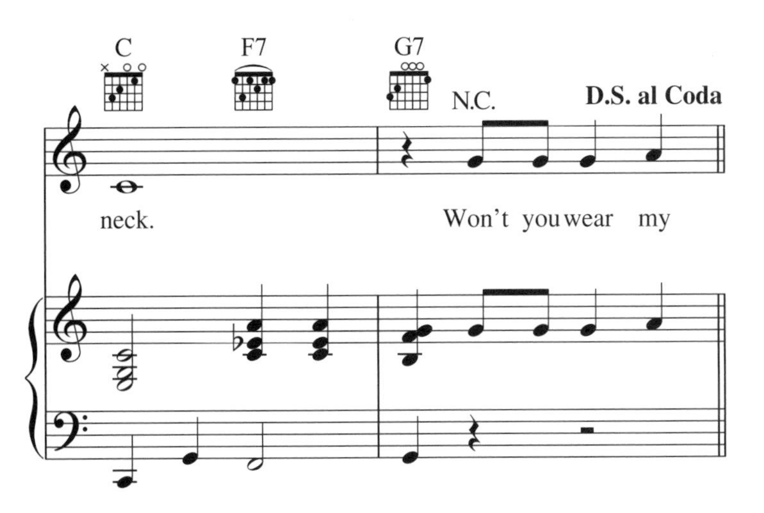
C
F7
G7
N.C.
D.S. al Coda
neck.
Won't you wear my

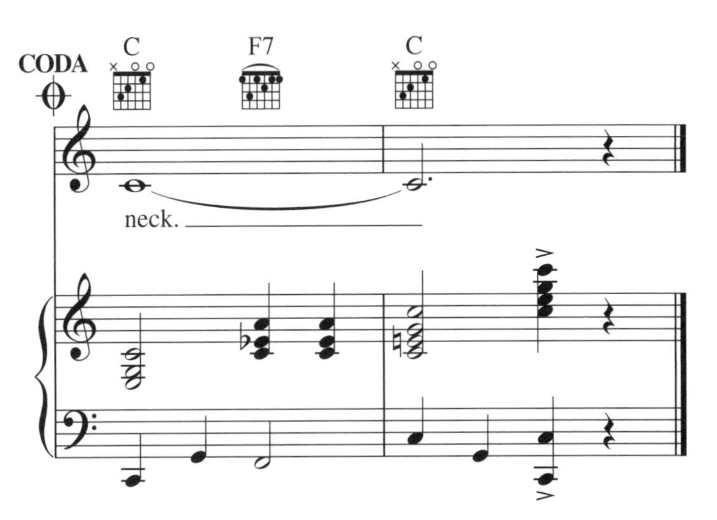
CODA
C
F7
C
neck.

TOO MUCH

Words and Music by LEE ROSENBERG
and BERNARD WEINMAN

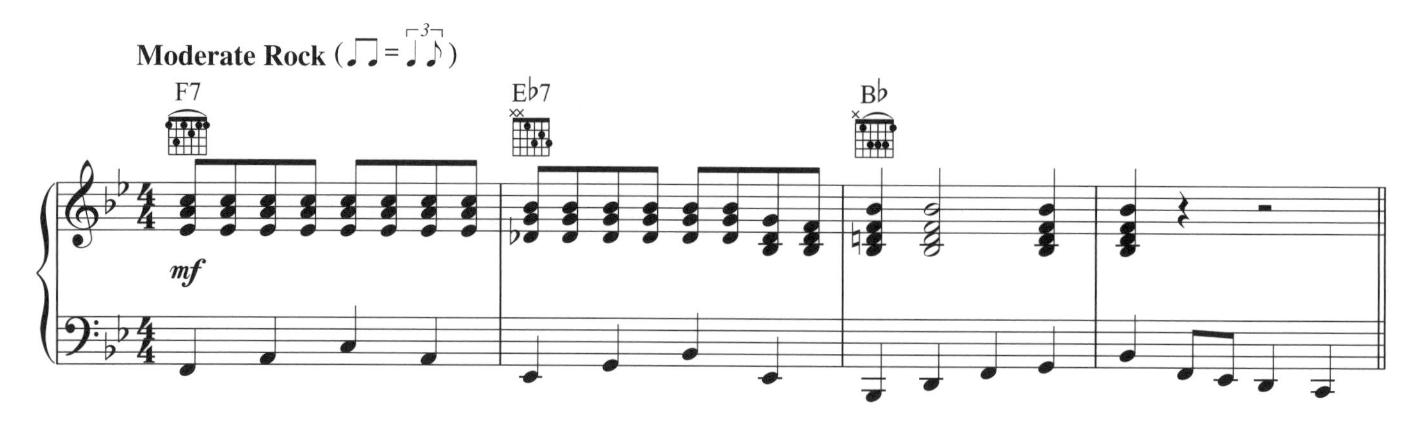

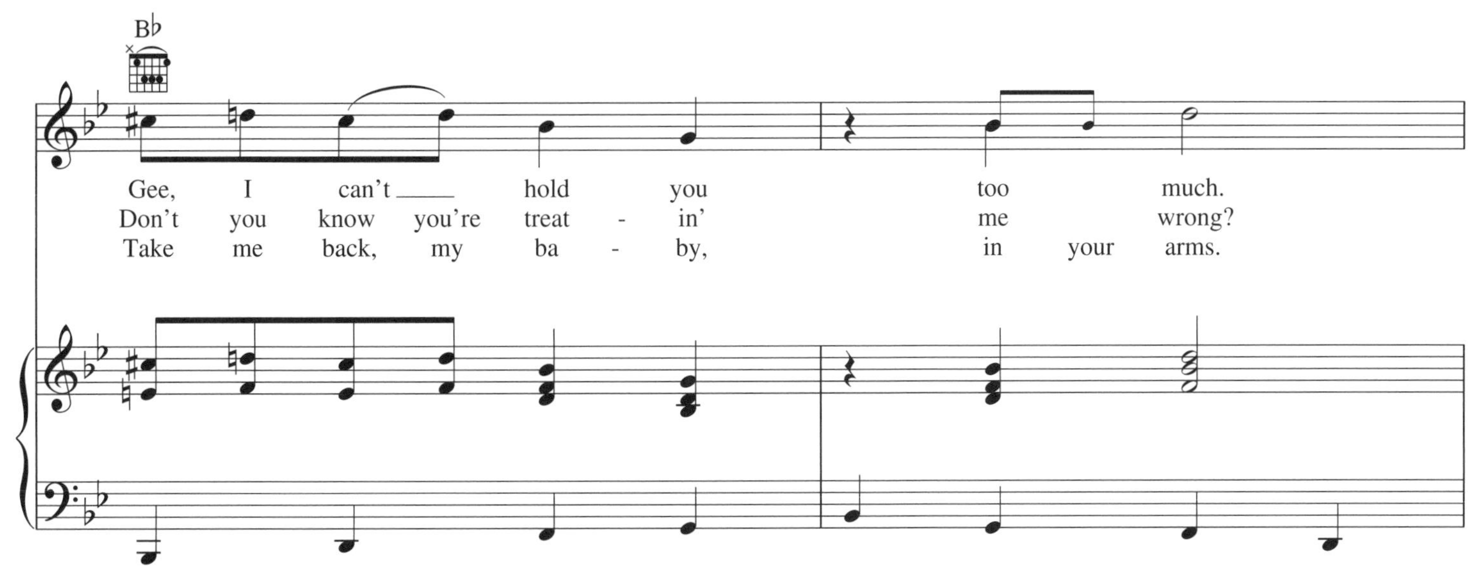
B♭
Gee, I can't hold you too much.
Don't you know you're treat - in' me wrong?
Take me back, my ba - by, in your arms.

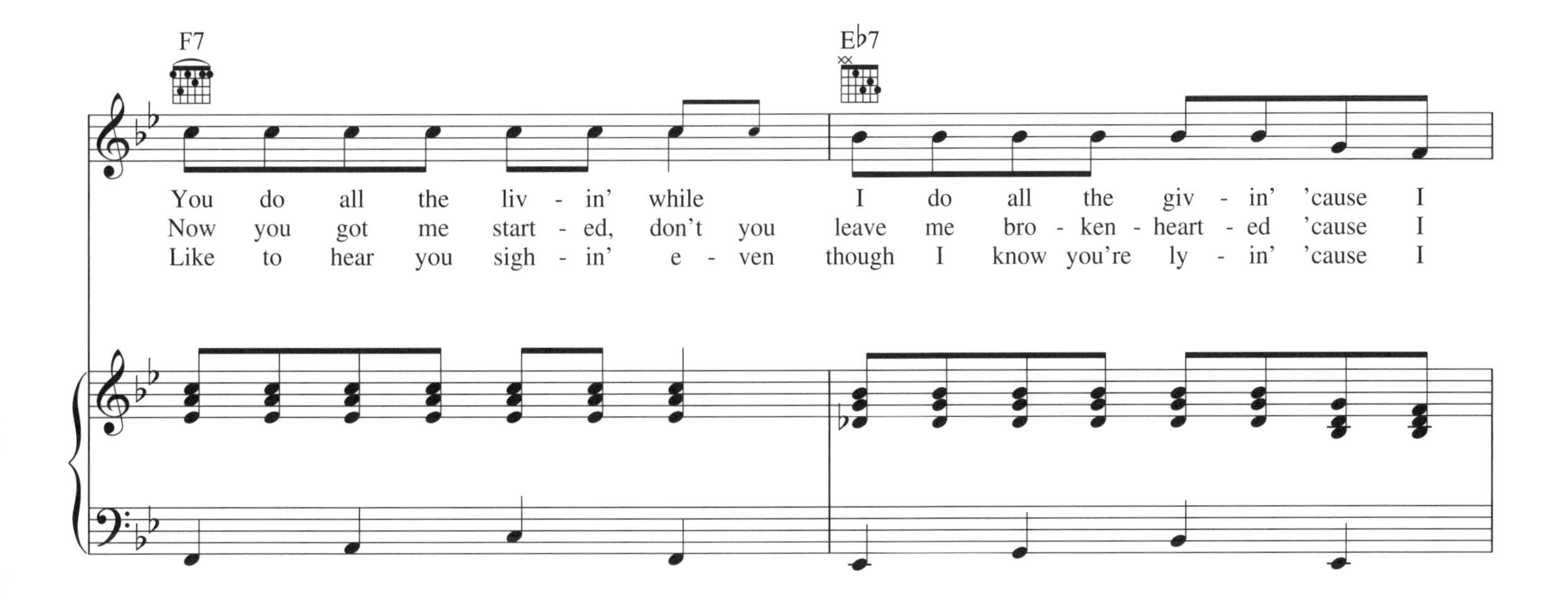
F7
E♭7
You do all the liv - in' while I do all the giv - in' 'cause I
Now you got me start - ed, don't you leave me bro - ken - heart - ed 'cause I
Like to hear you sigh - in' e - ven though I know you're ly - in' 'cause I

B♭
1
2, 3
love you too much.
love you too much.
love you too much.
Need your lov - in'

all the time.
Need your hug - gin';
please, be mine.

E♭7
B♭
Need you near me;
stay real close.
Please, please, hear me,

F7
E♭7
you're the most.
Now you got me start - ed, don't you
leave me bro - ken-heart - ed 'cause I

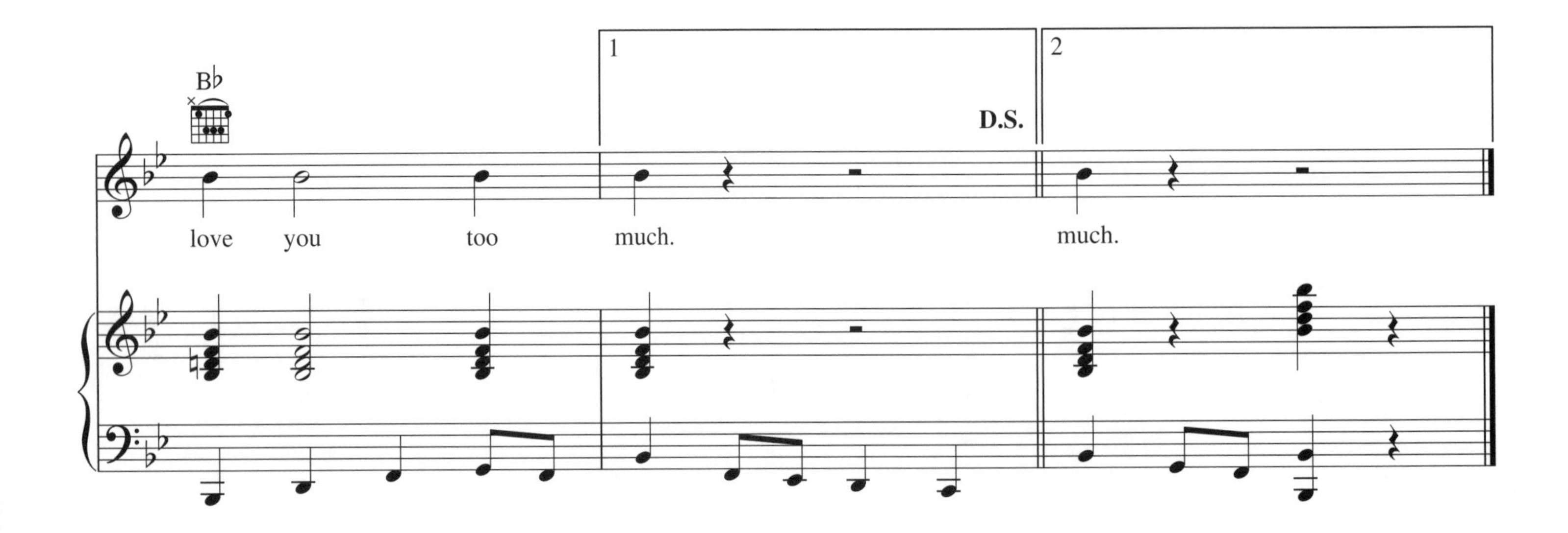
B♭
1
2
D.S.
love you too
much.
much.